Mom to Mom

HEART TO HEART

Mom to Mom

HEART TO HEART

Cari Haus & Sue Murray

REVIEW AND HERALD® PUBLISHING ASSOCIATION
HAGERSTOWN, MD 21740

The authors assume full responsibility for the accuracy of all facts
and quotations as cited in this book.

This book was
Edited by Richard W. Coffen
Designed by Patricia S. Wegh
Illustrations by Mary Bausman
Typeset: 11/13 Goudy

PRINTED IN U.S.A.

99 98 97 96   5 4 3 2 1

R&H Cataloging Service
Haus, Cari Hoyt
    Mom to mom: heart to heart, by
Cari Haus and Sue Murray.

    1. Motherhood.   2. Parenting.   3. Child rearing.
I. Murray, Sue, joint author.   II. Title.

306.8743

ISBN 0-8280-1306-6

Dedication

This book
is lovingly dedicated
to our husbands,
David and Don,
with whom we have shared
our parenting journeys,
and whose love
and encouragement
will always be appreciated,

and to our children,
Michael and Matthew
Marci and Ryan

who provided much of the inspiration
for this book.

Contents

Contents

Introduction

DEAR READERS:

Probably every mother needs someone to talk to about her parenting experiences and the challenges along the way. As a young mother, I have found a number of invaluable ideas through conversations with my friends, mother, and grandmother.

One of my best "mother mentors," as well as a dear friend, has been Sue Murray. Sue and I have worked together as coeditors of *Creative Parenting* for probably four or five years now. We also collaborated on a 220-page parenting resource entitled *Prime Time for Parents.* And now this book.

An integral part of our working relationship has been the verbal "side trips" we often take over the telephone. It's not at all unusual for me to share my latest parenting experience (or escapade, as the case may be!) with Sue. In turn, she oftens relates something that happened to her. And sometimes—especially when I ask—she shares some of the insights she has gained not only from her own parenting experiences but also in her career as a family life professional.

Now we have chosen to share some of those experiences with you—in a way that will (hopefully) provide good, helpful information and also catch the chemistry of our friendship. In letter form, I have written to Sue about some of my most meaningful (and in many cases humorous) parenting experiences. She in turn has reciprocated in much the same way as we might have conversed over the telephone.

Besides our letters to each other, we've included some other things especially for you. Sometimes at the end of a chapter you will see a section entitled "From My Files" or "From My Perspective." "From My Files" includes information we have gleaned from other sources, whereas in "From My Perspective" the author expands on a thought or issue addressed in the main part of that chapter.

"Reflections" ends each chapter. These questions are for you to think about, write about, talk about. If you are using this book

It's not unusual for me to share my latest parenting experience (or escapade, as the case may be!).

as part of a study group, these reflective questions can be the basis of your group discussion following the reading of each chapter.

We pray that as you read this book you will be blessed as an individual, as a mother (if you are one), and as a child of God. We hope that you will find

✔ a wealth of practical information you can use in meeting the experiences motherhood may bring your way.

✔ a new appreciation for the power of friendship and mentoring, which may even translate into a desire to cultivate new sharing relationships with the other mothers in your life.

✔ a new respect for the almost lost art of letter writing and a possible revival of that skill in your own life.

✔ a closer relationship to Jesus Christ, the world's foremost mentor, who had a cherished relationship with His own mother and who desires to have a personal relationship with every person today.

Chapter 1

SNAKES IN MY LAP

Hi Sue!

How are things down in your neck of the woods? If you answer "Boring!" you should move to Cedar Lake! (You'll understand that statement better after I update you on my latest adventure as a mom.)

I needed a break last week—and took it—leaving the kids with David for an hour or so. During my "mom's time off" excursion, which just happened to consist of driving to the grocery store and back *by myself*, a young friend dropped by our house. Seems he had just completed an excursion of sorts himself—a highly successful rummage for reptiles in his backyard.

Since David is a biology teacher, any beast found or sighted—dead or alive—with even the slightest degree of biological interest, is promptly reported to him. In this case, the find consisted of six baby snakes. The finder, a budding biologist himself, loaded his catch into a canning jar, flashed it in front of a few female friends, then generously offered it to David, who accepted.

When I returned (quite unsuspecting) from my shopping trip, who should greet me but Matthew . . . clasping a canning jar full of snakes!

"Look, Mommy!" he shouted. "Six baby snakes! Want to see?"

Needing a moment to regain my composure, I sank into our cushy couch to evaluate my less than numerous available options.

But before I could even plot phase one of a graceful retreat, Matthew pressed the jar of snakes onto my lap.

I was in the process of cautiously reaching out my hand to steady the jar when *bingo*—the top popped off! Before I could even muster a blood-curdling scream, six exhilarated (and liberated) baby snakes slithered happily onto my skirt, down my legs, and onto the living room floor.

We all screamed at David to catch them (from our perch on the couch, of course). And believe me, he tried! Being rather quick and well-coordinated, he had but one problem on his hands—snakes are quicker! And they all slithered in different directions.

"A child must touch, feel, see, taste, smell, hear, and . . . spill a little milk (or a few snakes) in order to grow."

11

Under the couch. Into the closet. Toward the stereo.

Despite their slithering efforts, he did collar four of the convoluting creatures in a matter of minutes. But a garter snake and one other unidentified reptile remained at large!

David really got a charge out of the whole situation. "Could be anywhere," he said with a smirk. "Down a heat duct, under the couch, or in our bed!" (Can you imagine!) "And it could be awhile till we find them," he went on to inform me. "After all, a snake that was missing from the biology room for two months finally did show up in the home economics room." (Much to the teacher's delight, as you can imagine.)

Now, I like going barefoot—especially in my house. But not if I think a baby snake might be nestled in every square foot of carpet. So I wore my slippers for a whole week!

Oh, by the way, we finally found them (the snakes, that is). They were dead. Unbeknownst to me, one had cozied up in my laundry! He was washed and dried before I even knew he was there! Snake number two expired on his way down to the laundry. He may have wanted a bath too. Guess I'll never know.

As a biology teacher's wife, I've entertained a number of strange guests in my home, but the six snakes in my lap will definitely go down as one of my more memorable experiences.

This whole thing got me thinking about appropriate pets—and I remembered something we edited in *Prime Time for Parents* awhile back—(remember?). I'll put it after this letter just in case you don't.

Then again, maybe there's some other hidden meaning behind this experience—just waiting to be uncovered. (Maybe you can enlighten me!)

Keep an eye on your canning jars,

Cari

> *"Anybody can make hay while the sun shines. I need to do my best while whistling in the dark."*

Found in My Files

"My advice to women? Don't mother anything with whiskers." Ruth Bryan Hudson

"Anybody who doesn't know what soap tastes like never washed a dog." Franklin P. Jones in *Quote Magazine*

"No symphony orchestra ever played music like a 2-year-old girl laughing with a puppy." Bern Williams in *National Enquirer*

"Cosmic upheaval is not so moving as a little child ponder-

ing the death of a sparrow in the corner of a barn." Thomas
Savage, *Her Side of It* (Little, Brown)

The following ideas are some shared in "Is Your House Like
Noah's Ark?" in *Prime Time for Parents*:

✓ Whether you like it or not, at some time your child is likely
to ask to keep a pet—or many pets!

✓ By matching the pet to your child's interests and age, you
may provide entertainment, a sense of growing responsibility,
and an awareness of God's infinite variety.

✓ Owning and caring for a pet can be one of the most genuinely rewarding experiences of childhood. Studies have revealed
that children with pets tend to be more empathetic and calmer
than their contemporaries who are without pets. Shy children
may become more communicative after having a pet they are
knowledgeable about.

✓ Caring for a pet helps develop a sense of nurturing and
tenderness.

✓ Small children should not be made responsible for the total
care and managing of an animal, but they can play an active role in
the care and feeding. Toddlers can often be unintentionally rough
with animals, so it is wise to have their interactions well-supervised.

✓ When considering a pet for your home, you may want to
take into consideration all aspects of the proposed pet's needs,
and observe your child around animals to make sure he or she is
not frightened or allergic before choosing a pet. (From *Prime
Time for Parents*)

REFLECTIONS

1. Can you identify with Solomon's counsel? "Do not boast
about tomorrow, for you do not know what a day may bring forth"
(Prov. 17:1, NIV). Do you have a snake story to tell?

2. What are your memories of childhood pets/animals? Do
you feel positive about having pets in your home?

3. Would periodic trips to the farm, zoo, or nature center be
just as beneficial for your child as having a pet?

4. What good things do you see happening for your child as
a result of having a pet, and what character traits would you like
your child to develop through the experience?

5. How could you handle your child's unnecessary roughness
or neglect of a pet?

Chapter 2

EXPECTING THE UNEXPECTED

Dear Cari,

I chuckled out loud as I read about your snakes! You made me want to put my slippers on too . . . and go check the laundry basket—just to be sure!

We found a snake in our bathtub once. What a shock! Ryan and Marci were quite intrigued, to say the least. They wanted to keep him, so I put him in a shoe box on top of our refrigerator. (I know that sounds like a strange home for a snake, but I thought that would keep him safe from the dog and cat.)

Unfortunately, when I went to get the box down to show the neighbors our "pet"—he was gone! What a creepy feeling!

We did find him later—with a small bite out of his side. And for whatever reason, he soon expired and we had a proper burial. I bet a lot of mothers have some version of a snake story!

I guess as mothers there is one thing we can be certain of—there will be surprises! Some surprises are short-lived (literally, like your six snakes); and some, like an unexpected pregnancy, have consequences of a much longer (and louder!) duration.

One day when several children were playing on the swing set in our yard, I heard a blood-curdling scream that nearly scared me to death! I raced outside, dreading the possibility that someone had been drastically hurt on *our* swing set! When I reached the children, only one child was screaming. She hadn't lost a limb, and she wasn't even bleeding; but I couldn't calm her enough to find out what was wrong. Then I saw the problem—a big, green bug in the lawn.

I could understand her being startled, even scared, by that big green bug. But her reaction was so intense! Several of the other children were immensely interested in the iridescent creature, but she was terrified! As I came to know this child better, I observed that she had other fearful tendencies that limited her enjoyment of the world around her, especially when it came to the things of nature. And as I came to know her mother better, I saw that the little girl was often a reflection of her mother's fears.

"If you're never scared or embarrassed or hurt, it means you never take any chances."

Julia Sorel,
See How She Runs
(Ballantine Books).

14

When those snakes landed in your lap, what a surprise! I was reflecting on your letter and thinking there are several reactions you could have had that Michael and Matthew would have observed and possibly imitated later. You could have

✓ come completely unglued and fallen apart—that would have been startling!

✓ threatened life and limb of all involved—loading on guilt for upsetting you.

✓ gone into seclusion for the rest of the day—more guilt and confusion.

If you had reacted that strongly, your boys might have also gotten the message that snakes are awful and scary; we must protect mommy from snakes (and lots of other things); and if she can't handle a surprise, we probably can't either. On the other hand, it's natural to be startled (and perhaps scared) of snakes and other unexpected reptiles, rodents, and whatever categories other creepy-crawlers fit into. And then there are other unpleasant surprises that land in our laps—like unexpected company, changes in work schedules we have to adjust to quickly, or finding one child who has just gotten a new haircut from another. The list could go on and on, but I think the point is that there is a myriad of life-events that startle us. Some of these surprises are delightful, but some are just plain shocking.

It seems to me that what's most important is not the surprises themselves, but how we react to them. We teach our children by our own responses to life's surprises.

When we see unexpected events as possibilities for growth, we can rejoice (and adjust). We can know it's OK to be scared of unexpected things. We can learn to adjust, to get over our fear if necessary. We can decide how we want to react to life's little surprises.

My experience has taught me that in parenting there will always be surprises—as well as lessons to be learned from them. We may be astonished or astounded at what lands in our lap. But just remember—even if we don't know what surprises tomorrow holds, there's one thing we can be certain of—we know Who holds tomorrow!

Should I take my slippers off now?

Sue

P.S. Here are some other interesting things I thought about surprises:

"When patterns are broken, new worlds can emerge."

Tuli Kupferberg

✔ What sometimes seems like a wonderful surprise to you may not be so wonderful to someone else. So we need to be sensitive before planning a surprise for someone that may not be such a sweet surprise to them.

✔ Reminiscing about surprising events that have happened in your family can help build family memories and provide security and reassurance for your children.

✔ Surprises can be the "spice of life." Planning surprises for those you love and care for is a vital part of building a strong family!

"Your expression is the most important thing you can wear."

Sid Ascher in
Pleasantville, N. J.
Mainland Journal

FOUND IN MY FILES

THE PARENT'S PLEDGE

✔ I will set a good example for my child.

✔ I will show my children I love them every day through words and physical affection.

✔ I will listen to my children and let them know I value what they say.

✔ I will praise my child's accomplishments and efforts towards accomplishments.

✔ I will have realistic expectations for my children. I will allow them to make their own mistakes and learn from those experiences.

✔ I will respect my children as individuals even if I don't always agree with them.

✔ I will enjoy my children and make time to share interests and appreciate one another.

✔ I will love my children unconditionally. I will let them know they are lovable, worthwhile, and valuable human beings. (The Bureau for At-Risk Youth, 645 New York Ave., Huntington, NY 11743; 1-800-99-YOUTH)

REFLECTIONS

1. What are some of the surprises you have had in your parenting experiences?

2. How do you feel about how you've handled some of these surprises?

3. Consider John 16:33: "I have told you these things, so that in me you may have peace. In this world you will have trou-

ble. But take heart! I have overcome the world" (NIV). In terms of surprises and unexpected events in your life, what does this text say to you?

4. What do you want your children to know about handling life's surprises? How are you teaching them?

5. What's something you would enjoy being surprised by?

"People judge you by your actions, not your intentions. You may have a heart of gold, but so does a hard-boiled egg."

Good Reading

LESSONS FROM A LIZARD

Hi again, Sue!

I've got another nature "nugget" for you. This one started at the post office, if you can imagine that.

"The brook would lose its song if you removed the rocks."

Last Saturday night I ran down to get the mail, expecting to pick up the usual pile of bills. Instead, the postmaster warily handed me a box labeled "LIVE CONTENTS, OPEN IMMEDIATELY!"

I have to admit that I've never gotten *anything* alive in the mail before! Being somewhat fearful to open the box myself (you never know what might jump out at you), I carried it dutifully home to David.

He was delighted! We had seven teenagers over for a party that evening, and they all got swept away by this unbridled enthusiasm to open the box.

"I think these might be the two gecko lizards I ordered." David grabbed *my bread knife* (can you imagine?) and sliced through the packing tape. "You probably saved their lives by going to the post office tonight," he said to me, "since they wouldn't have survived until Monday morning."

I felt honored to have done such a noble deed for the two poor, helpless lizards (well, kind of!). And upon their emergence from the box, the two geckos were immediately the life of the party.

Having never petted a lizard before, I didn't see any reason to get started at this late date in life. So I kept a cool distance and made an effort to act at least half as thrilled as everybody else in the room seemed to be.

Things got really exciting when one gecko escaped. His little reptilian brain evidently sensed that his last and only chance for freedom had arrived, and he went zigging and zagging across my living room floor!

There was a wild chase across the carpet—and with eight big kids (if you count my husband) plus two toddlers in hot pursuit of this hapless reptile, it's a wonder he didn't get stepped on!

Sensing the futility of his situation, he made a mad dash for—

and found—temporary asylum under the stereo cabinet! The students coaxed and prodded, and the next time the gecko made a run for the border one student was ready for him. He reached right out and grabbed him by the tail!

But that posed no problem for the fearless gecko. He just unhooked that tail and continued on his merry way! Can you believe that! His tail came right off and he was apparently no worse for the wear.

"Oh, don't worry!" David said. "He'll grow a new one!"

I hate to admit it, but I wasn't worried about whether or not he would grow a new one. I was just worried about how long he would remain at large in my living room (here we go with the slippers again).

Oh, I did learn an important biological fact from this experience—dropping off tails just happens to be a defense mechanism God created for geckos. They can survive just fine without it—and even grow a new one, although healing may take as long as a year.

You know, I think God has a plan for helping us handle loss as well as for healing after a loss—just like He has for the gecko lizard that lost his tail.

Cari

P. S. Thought for the day: You may speak of love and tenderness and passion, but real ecstasy is discovering that there's not a lizard loose in your house after all!

"Some people think it's holding on that makes one strong. Sometimes it's letting go."

Sylvia Robinson in *The Christian Science Monitor*

FROM MY PERSPECTIVE

Some points to ponder on "losing your tail"—

✓ God loves and cares for us. But God doesn't always intervene to protect us from the consequences of living in a sinful world.

✓ One of the greatest challenges to us as parents is to teach our children about God's love and care for them without teaching that God always intervenes to protect us from the results of living in a sinful world.

✓ We need to think and plan now how we will respond to questions we will inevitably face when our children experience a loss—even though they prayed for a different answer.

✓ One good thing to keep in mind when facing these issues is that when we give our lives to God, they are God's to protect

for eternity! We may suffer loss on this messed-up planet, but because of God's sacrifice for us, our ability to experience the ultimate—eternal life—is never in doubt!

REFLECTIONS

1. What can we learn from the lizards' ability to lose and regrow a tail? Can we learn lessons about healing or loss through nature?

2. Have you ever suffered a loss from which you begged God to spare you? How did you feel?

3. Have you seen God directly protect you or a loved one from danger? How did you feel?

4. Have you ever wondered why God protects you from loss sometimes but not at other times?

Chapter 4

HOW TO KEEP RUNNING
AFTER YOU LOSE YOUR TAIL

Dear Cari:

Are you sure it's a good idea for you to go to the post office? I wasn't sure whom to commiserate with—you or the gecko! It certainly would have been interesting to be at your house that Saturday night.

It's too bad the gecko had to lose his tail. But what's really neat is that God has a plan in motion to take care of the gecko's loss—even before it happens. And also that even though healing is possible, it usually takes time.

That thought can be very reassuring for us when it comes to loss, pain, and hurting. Not knowing much (almost nothing, really) about geckos, I'm not sure if it hurt him to lose that tail. But in human terms I know loss hurts! Pain is pain! Sometimes we deny our pain, because it's not as awful as we think someone else's is. But anyone who has had a paper cut knows how painful that can be! When the initial sting of a paper cut has eased, I usually try to discount the injury because it's just a paper cut. But if I don't tend to that cut, it usually flares up, and I'm painfully reminded every time something comes into contact with my finger.

My experience has been that pain is just a part of life. There's only one book from which I remember the first line, other than the Bible verse I memorized from Genesis 1:1. That's M. Scott Peck's book, *The Road Less Traveled*. His first line reads: "Life is difficult." When I read that, it wasn't news to me, but I just didn't want to hear it. I didn't really want to read on, but the book was assigned reading for a class I was taking, so I did. It turned out that Peck was saying more than just "life is difficult." Peck was also saying that there are no easy answers. This seems to be especially true when it comes to loss or pain (like the lizard losing his tail, for example).

I've observed that each person reacts very differently to pain. Some run, some deny, some wallow in it, and some fight back. Unfortunately, unresolved pain can keep us from being complete and content people. We may not even be aware of

"A dead goldfish. A broken jelly glass. They may not seem like much to the rest of the world, but life's smaller sorrows deserve to be mourned."

Barbara Bartocci

21

that pain on a daily basis, but when someone rubs up against that hurtful place, we react!

But painful experiences can also bring about positive things. For example, they give us the opportunity to reexamine our life. When my children were much younger, I became aware that I was being very much affected (much more than a paper cut!) by the pain of a certain relationship. I was carrying around some unanswered questions, frustration, hurt, and even anger; and these burdens were becoming so heavy that I was being influenced more than I had wanted to admit.

As I examined my hurt and pain, I realized I was operating from a message that I'd internalized: if you love God, and study and pray enough, you shouldn't have problems in relationships. I guess I thought that if I was really filled with the Holy Spirit, my emotions should always be in good order and I could be in a good relationship with anyone. And so it was all up to me.

But I couldn't seem to fix this situation. In my quiet moments I began to realize that too much of my energy was being used trying to do the impossible, and I had less and less energy for my family. They needed me at my best! Yes, I had to accept appropriate responsibility in the relationship, but it wasn't all up to me. So I wrote one of the most difficult letters of my life. In that letter I shared my perception of the situation, that I wanted to continue in the relationship, but that I needed to give my best energies to my husband and children. I could no longer carry the total responsibility for the difficulties in our relationship.

The potential for loss was there, but I had to take the risk. It was incredibly scary to fold that letter, address the envelope, and drop it into the mailbox. I wasn't used to being so direct and addressing difficult issues. I had long lived with some rules I had learned as a child, such as "Don't rock the boat" and "Don't talk about difficult things." Yet somehow when that letter was on it's way, I began to feel a gentle sense of peace, a letting go of the past. Yes, I had to put some expectations aside, and even though the act of losing something was painful, I also began to heal. I literally felt a surge of physical and emotional energy. I remember calling to Marci and Ryan, and when they came to me I hugged and kissed them and told them how much I loved them, how much I enjoyed being their mother. They didn't really understand what was going on (but they liked it).

After that decision, I had a new kind of energy to use to com-

"We shouldn't wallow in self-pity, but every so often, it's OK to swish our feet a little."

Cartoon caption

mit to my family. I guess in one way (like the gecko) I began to grow a new tail. Of course, there was still some pain and grief and adjustment. But I was freed to go on, to not be burdened down by something I had little control over. I learned that I could control my own emotions and reactions, but I could not be responsible for someone else's decisions. To some degree, in facing my loss, I also found freedom.

It's interesting that you said it takes almost a year for the gecko's tail to heal. So even though God gave the gecko this terrific mechanism to heal and regenerate, it doesn't happen overnight. I believe God gives us the same power to heal and regenerate—although healing from loss, like growth, doesn't take place overnight for us either.

Well, those are some deep thoughts in exchange for a gadabout gecko tale! Take care, and think twice before your next trip to the post office!

Sue

FROM MY PERSPECTIVE

When we are living with loss and pain, many of us try to live in isolation. The time that we need others the most is the time when we have a greater tendency to withdraw. But in doing this we sabotage ourselves. Without the comfort and love of other human beings, we suffer even greater loss. Grieving involves searching, risk-taking, sharing our pain. Sometimes we even hesitate to do this with God. But it needs to be done, and it needs to be done in our own time. Generally in our American society we get the message that we "should get over it," "get on with the rest of our lives," "lay it to rest." But with loss and pain, comes grief.

Sometimes we need to say, "Don't take my grief away from me." The reality is that it takes a minimum of six months to a year for healing from any significant loss (about the time it takes a gecko to grow a new tail). Some aspects of grieving will continue into the second year and even longer. It depends on many things, like the circumstances of the loss and what the loss means to each person. In the case of losing another person, we are affected by any "unfinished" business we had with that person.

There are different types of people we may look to for comfort and friendship in times of pain, loss, and grief.

"I have wasted much time on vain regrets— in fact, that's one of my biggest regrets."

Ashleigh Brilliant

23

"The human

heart does

not stay

away too

long from

that which

hurt it most.

There is

a return

journey to

anquish that

few of us

are released

from

making."

Lillian Smith

✓ Empathetic caring persons

Empathetic caring persons will be good listeners. Even though they may have different views or values from ours, they won't shame or judge us. These people can be fully trusted. They are not embarrassed by our tears, they don't shock easily, and they listen to and accept our feelings. They don't regularly give unwanted advice, are warm and affectionate, and remind us of our strengths when we have forgotten we have these strengths within us. Empathetic persons trust us to be able to come through our difficult time. They aren't afraid of our questions, respect our courage, and are faithful to their commitments and promises. They understand that grief is not a disease.

✓ Assertive Caring Persons

Assertive caring persons are more likely to respond to practical concerns. Although they respect our need for privacy, they won't ignore our need for human contact. They volunteer to help out with tasks that are too difficult for us. They help us think things over aloud. They provide tangible things like food and child care. They treat our belongings with care and keep confidential whatever personal information we share. They tend to focus more on reducing the stress, and they care for us in practical ways that are comforting and helpful.

✓ Unhelpful Persons

Unhelpful persons may be charming and likable. You may have shared good times together and consider them close. Yet somehow these persons lack the ability to support and care for you in the ways you need. They may actually complicate your journey of dealing with your pain. They may tell others things you intended to have kept in confidence, tell you stories of tragedy and catastrophe when you are vulnerable, and make light of things sacred or meaningful to you. They question your decisions, respond in ways that are poorly timed or are somehow unsettling, and continue behaviors you have identified as being hurtful to you. These people fail to follow through on promises and may label your feelings or behaviors as "weird," "hysterical," "childish," "selfish," or "just feeling sorry for yourself."

If persons are more destructive than caring and helpful, you need to ask yourself why you are continuing in this relationship. Don't continue to rely on this type person because you aren't sure anyone else would care for you. There *are* others. Friends can be found in unlikely places and in all age groups.

And then sometimes we do need to put our pain aside to be available for helping others. Most good friendships and love relationships are like this. People take turns. It's not fair to look to one person to meet all our needs, and people can't really know what we need from them unless we tell them. Many operate from the "If they really loved me . . ." myth. That's when our thinking says, "If they really loved me, they would know what to do . . . what to say . . . or what I need . . . without my having to ask."

We must each seek our own way when we've lost our tail; but God will be there beside us, and others want to be too.

REFLECTIONS

1. Has there been a time in your life when God's plan was in motion to take care of your need before you realized it?

2. Is there something you need to let go of so that you can grow?

3. Are you carrying some pain that is keeping you from giving your best energies to your family? If so, what can you do?

4. Who is there that could or will support you as you work through your pain or loss?

5. How would you describe yourself in relating to others in pain?

Chapter 5

TUB GRINDER, ANYONE?

Dear Sue,

"The philosopher who said that work well done never needs doing over probably never had kids."

You'll never guess what Matthew wanted to buy today! It's called a "tub grinder." I just happened to be looking at a tub grinder catalogue when he got the bright idea.

Just for the record, a tub grinder is a rather impressive-looking piece of machinery (bigger than my house) with a cab on one end and a tub on the other. It has one colossal set of claws, which the operator uses to pick up all kinds of debris. The claws throw the trash in the tub, where it is ground to powder. Looking at tub grinder catalogues is not a hobby of mine—I just happened to be doing an article for the local newspaper on the company that makes them. But buying a tub grinder for ourselves—now that was an inspiration! Matthew must have noticed the incredulous look on my face when he said we should buy one.

"Guess we already have a lawn mower," he chirped, just as cheerily. I just sat there, thinking about what a massive piece of machinery these tub grinders were. The manufacturer bragged that they could "process" between 75 and 100 tons of debris an hour. Why, tub grinders had even been used to clean up after Hurricane Andrew.

"Debris," I mumbled. That's when it hit me. I sat still for a moment, overwhelmed at the house-cleaning possibilities of a mini-tub grinder in my home. I know that tub grinders are usually reserved for major disaster areas, but hey, who's to decide what qualifies? I wondered if the tub grinder company had ever thought of other uses for their equipment.

I hate to admit this, but my home often looks like it got hit by not one but two hurricanes. (Their names are Matthew and Michael.)

One of my more embarrassing moments was several years ago when a certain 6-year-old (who shall remain nameless) visited our home. Our house may have been messier than usual right at that moment—I really can't remember. But I do remember her candor. She looked at me with these big blue and very innocent eyes and asked sweetly, "Is your house always this messy, or do you clean it for Sabbath?"

I usually manage to see the humor in such situations, and I informed her quite gravely that I did indeed clean my house every week, and no, it was not always this messy!

Since then, I have come across a book that has been quite helpful. It is called *The Messie's Manual*, and by reading this book I learned that I was actually born a "messie"—without even the slightest chance to possibly be a "cleanie."

This doesn't mean that being a messie is part of my nature and I am no longer responsible for my actions. It does mean that organization might not come naturally for me—although it can be learned! And what is even more amazing was that I learned that most messies are actually perfectionists about their housecleaning.

When I first mentioned my newfound knowledge to my mother, a die-hard cleanie, she didn't say anything. She laughed. But I've learned to ignore this cleanie incredulity. Because it's true. If I go to clean up something, I want to do it right. If there's not time to do that, I don't do it at all.

So I had to undergo a basic attitude adjustment. One of my cleanie friends showed me one of her secrets of an orderly home— what she calls the "Swiss Cheese Method of Housecleaning."

You just imagine you are a mouse (yes, I know they are rodents), confronted with a big piece of cheese (or monumental task, which is more likely to be the case). You just keep nibbling away at it, and guess what? Before you know it, the piece of cheese is not so large anymore.

The Messie's Manual had its own name tag for a new version of keeping house—the "Mount Vernon Method of Housecleaning" (first utilized not by George Washington, but by the people who cleaned his historic home). In the Mount Vernon Method, you start at your front door and work around the wall of each room—straightening as you go. If something interrupts you, you make a mental note of where you left off and pick up right there in the next session. The trick here is to distinguish between straightening and cleaning. If you do a full-scale cleaning the first time, you may never get past the first wall. So you do the straightening first, and when that is accomplished, you come back for another, more in-depth run.

The beauty of this method is that you can actually see you are making progress through the house, rather than working the

"One of the advantages of being disorderly is that one is constantly making exciting discoveries."

A. A. Milne

27

"here a little, there a little—doesn't look like I did anything" method of house cleaning I had used for so long. From personal experience, I can testify that the Mount Vernon as well as the Swiss cheese methods of housecleaning do work. My house is not spotless, or even close to it, but I have seen significant improvements after using these methods.

Cari

P.S. Here's a touch of encouragement (or discouragement, depending on your perspective) for those of us who want a new start sometimes: "Today is the first day of the rest of your life—unless you live on the other side of the international dateline, in which case yesterday was the first day of the rest of your life." Orben's *Current Comedy*

"It is one of life's unchanging laws: All friendly dogs have dirty paws."

Barbara Rhodes
in *The Wall Street Journal*

FOUND IN MY FILES

Important definitions for housecleaning moms to know from *The Mom Dictionary*:

Bathroom: A room used by the entire family, believed by all except Mom to be self-cleaning.

Carpet: Expensive floor covering used to catch spills and to clean mud off shoes.

Hamper: A wicker container with a lid, usually surrounded by, but not containing, dirty clothing.

Handi-wipes: Pants, shirt-sleeves, drapes, etc.

Tips for a cleaner house; gleaned from *The Messie's Manual*:

✓ If your house looks like a hurricane hit it, remember: Your house did not get this way overnight, so it will not become clean overnight. Make it a priority, set reasonable goals and it will happen!

✓ If you feel discouraged about the condition of your home, do not give up trying. According to *The Messie's Manual*, she "who aims at nothing, is likely to hit it."

✓ If, when trying the Mount Vernon Method of cleaning, you just happen to run into an area of your house considered too tough to tackle, take a day off, then go for it and then reward yourself with a little something extra-special when you finish the big bad job.

✓ Try posting and following the "Rules of the House":

If you open it—close it.
If you get it out—put it away.
If you sleep in it—make it up.
If you drink out of it—wash it.
If you take it off—hang it up.
If you turn it on—turn it off.
If you drop it—pick it up.
If you clip it—file it.
If it hurts—comfort it.
If it cries—love it.

✓ Enlist the family's help.

REFLECTIONS

1. Would you be best described as a "cleanie" or a "messie"? Are you comfortable with who you are when it comes to housecleaning?

2. Do you give your family the impression that having a clean house is more important than they are? Or are you more interested in other projects than you are in your house?

3. What housecleaning tips or methods have worked for you in the past?

4. What new ideas would you like to try?

5. How can you get your family involved?

Chapter 6

KEEPING A SPOTLESS HOUSE
(AND OTHER FASCINATING FICTION)

Dear Cari:

"Children certainly brighten up a home. Did you ever see a child under 12 turn off an electric light?"

Unknown

Wow! Your letter reminded me of that statement about "cleanliness being next to godliness," and it really struck home! When I went away to a boarding high school, I learned all about that creed. I remember a picture in the yearbook from my sophomore year. With a big institutional polisher, I am buffing the freshly waxed outdoor, tiled front entry to the administration building of the school. When I first went there, I worked as a janitor, and that was part of my job on Friday. Every other Sunday morning we, on our hands and knees, cleaned and polished the entire floor of the chapel—with seats for 500. Can you believe it?

In the dormitory, our rooms were checked daily. We had random checks for dust on the bed springs, dust on the top of the door jams, even dust on the little top knobs of the door hinges! And I could tell you more! I learned how to clean like I never had before.

Then I went to college and majored in home economics. For an exam in household management class we had to plot the most efficient patterns of movement for all household tasks. For example, we had to show the traffic pattern for vacuuming an entire house. To this day, when I vacuum I mentally plot out how to be the most efficient. It bugs me to death, but some things are not easily forgotten!

By nature I do things rather logically (at least to my way of thinking), and I had expectations of the way a "professional home economist" should keep her home. The reality wasn't so easy. Someone has said: "The trouble with life is it's so daily." Well, the trouble with housecleaning is that *it's* so daily!

And the more people in the house, the merrier! When thinking of a man and a woman and a house, I remember hearing about a situation a young couple encountered on their first night of marriage. He changed by the bed that night, dropped his underwear on the floor, and hopped into bed.

When he and his new wife got ready to leave the next morn-

30

ing, the underwear was still there. He didn't think it was his job to pick it up. She didn't think it was her job to pick it up. In his family, his mother always picked up the underwear. In her family, her father always took care of his own underwear.

Would you believe that they were both so stubborn that in a couple of days they had to buy him new underwear? (Myself, I would have given in to save the money!) This became such an issue with them that they eventually went to a counselor. The counselor helped them work out a compromise. If a laundry hamper was purchased and placed in the bathroom or bedroom, would he be willing to put his underwear there? If it was placed in the hamper, would she be willing to take it from the hamper to the washer?

Tongue in cheek, I'd say they had a "brief" problem.

Our doorbell rings often (more often than most can imagine), and I never know who will be at the door. It seemed like when the children were little, the bell always rang when I was changing, feeding, bathing, or getting a little one to sleep. It also rings when the place is a mess! I decided a long time ago not to apologize for the state of affairs in my home. I adopted the view that my real friends don't care, and my enemies won't believe me anyway! (It's not that I have real enemies, but what I'm saying is that people who are committed to be supportive of me aren't going to withdraw their friendship, support, care, or concern because my house is a mess!)

It has been difficult not to try to be the perfect homemaker and put pressure on everyone to have everything always picked up. A sense of order and cleanliness is important to me, but not more important than the people who live in my home or who are at my door.

I remember someone telling me that when her children were young, she cleaned the kitchen floor, on her hands and knees, four times a day: after breakfast, after lunch, after dinner, and then a quick clean-up at night before she went to bed. I do admire someone having that kind of energy! But I've wondered what messages she was giving to her family. (That they always needed to be cleaned-up after? That they messed up her life?)

Now that we are empty-nested, I realize that clutter and dirt just happen. No longer can I say it's because there are kids in the house. As parents, we probably attribute more of the dirt and mess to the kids than they deserve. I'm also realizing how much

"The . . . trouble with cleaning the house is it gets dirty the next day anyway. So, skip a week if you have to. The children are the most important thing."

Barbara Bush

assistance Marci and Ryan really were. They were helpers from the beginning! I have a snapshot of Marci when she was barely walking, helping take clothes out of the dryer and putting them into the laundry basket. There's another picture of her when she was a bit older, proudly showing off how she set the table all by herself! Another "Kodak moment" is Ryan grinning ear-to-ear, so proud that he had carried the trash outside and dumped it in the big trash barrel. They weren't always that enthusiastic, but the memories were encouraging later on!

Don't get me wrong. It wasn't easy to stay on top of things, and we didn't have the perfectly spick-and-span clean house. But one strategy I used when it seemed like I had worked on the house all morning and it still wasn't clean or neat was to set a timer for 10 minutes and do as much as I could do in each room during that amount of time. It was amazing what I could accomplish in six areas of the house in just one hour. It really helped motivate the kids too. Another thing I tried—and I still do this—was to do a drawer a day. My tendency is to get into really huge projects, which leave me with a bigger mess. But when I tackle just one drawer each day and give myself the freedom to do just that one drawer, the task is manageable—and so is my attitude!

We did decide to be "equal opportunity employers," so there was no "woman's work" or "man's work" at our house—it was anyone and everyone's work. As the kids got older, another thing we did was to post a list on the refrigerator of all the things that needed to be done each day or during the week. Each person decided what he or she would be responsible for. It's amazing how much easier it is to do something when we have some ownership for it, and have had some choices!

The bottom line is this: until heaven we'll both have homes that need to be cleaned! If you find a household model of a tub grinder, let me know; I could still use one!

Sue

P.S. A friend and I were having a heart-to-heart conversation over dessert in a restaurant not long ago. We were sharing some of our experiences during the past twenty-some years, in particular the challenges of marriage and parenting. She, a mother of five, was saying that she's been discouraged because it doesn't seem as if she has lived up to the counsel she's read about being a good wife and mother. When she referred to the woman described in Proverbs 31, I responded by saying, "Well, I think that the illustration in Proverbs 31 is a model of all the potential things we can accomplish throughout the course of a lifetime. We don't have to do it all in two weeks!"

And she exclaimed, "Two weeks! I thought I was supposed to get it all done in a day."

We laughed and laughed, but the reality of trying to live up to that model on a daily basis is no laughing matter!

HOW TO MAKE A CAKE

Light oven; get out utensils and ingredients. Remove blocks and toy autos from table. Grease pan, crack nuts.

Measure two cups of flour; remove Johnny's hands from flour; wash flour off him. Remeasure flour.

Put flour, baking powder, and salt in sifter. Get dustpan and brush up pieces of bowl Johnny knocked on floor. Get another bowl. Answer doorbell.

Return to kitchen. Remove Johnny's hands from bowl. Wash Johnny. Answer phone. Return. Remove 1/4 inch salt from greased pan. Look for Johnny. Grease another pan. Answer telephone.

Return to kitchen and find Johnny. Remove his hands from bowl. Take up greased pan, and find layer of nutshells in it. Head for Johnny, who flees, knocking bowl off table.

Wash kitchen floor, table, walls, dishes. Call the baker. Lie down. (Author unknown)

OUT OF THE MOUTHS OF BABES

From "Concerning Mom and Her Housekeeping Habits" in *My Mother Is the Best Gift I Ever Got* by David Heller:

"My opinion is that a neat house is a boring house. . . . Of course, my mother has a different opinion." **Tom, age 10**

"My mother is weird. She thinks that cleaning the house is the greatest thing since sliced bread." **James, age 10**

"She is a neat freak. I think she needs to take up knitting so she'll calm down." **Rachel, age 8**

"She makes up a name for every room that we got to clean. Mine is 'Operation Disaster.'" **Jan, age 8**

REFLECTIONS

1. Are you ever stubborn about the way you do some things? What are the results?

2. If you could invent an appliance or cleaning apparatus, what would it be?

3. What messages are you giving your family about your values for your home?

4. What does Proverbs 31 mean to you?

Chapter 7

THE TALE OF TWO RODENTS
(THAT WERE GUESTS IN MY HOME)

Dear Sue,

Can you bear one more animal story? I just got back from the post office the other day (I can hear you saying, "Oh no! Not the post office again!") to find two furry creatures caged in my son's room. (In case you haven't noticed, the post office is the social hub in Cedar Lake *and* my five-minutes-away-from-the-kids-in-many-a-busy-day. It's also the place I usually am when "trouble" starts at home.)

In this case, the trouble happened to be two large rats that had moved in the minute I vacated the house.

"Aren't they cute?" Matthew was asking.

I stopped mentally scolding myself for going to the post office and tried to respond appropriately. "Cutest rats I ever saw."

"The new pastor just brought them over." David was quick to share the blame. "He has two boys, but they don't want the rats anymore. They thought we might like to have them."

"How generous." I could hardly conceal my pleasure! "When I meet this new pastor, I'll have to let him know how grateful I am," I mumbled under my breath. Out loud, I said, "Well, what shall we name them—Michael and Matthew?"

Michael immediately caught the somewhat uncomplimentary nature of my suggestion, and responded in kind. "How about Mommy and Daddy?"

I gave him a withering look, then softened a little when I realized that calling the rats "Michael and Matthew" was also a rather insulting thing to do.

"They already have names," David was saying. "Roland and Samuel, after the pastor's boys."

"Let's just keep those names," Michael suggested.

I have to admit that we never did figure out which rat was Roland and which was Samuel, but Roland and Samuel they were.

There was just one problem with Roland and Samuel. Michael and Matthew seemed to have trouble remembering to put the lid back on the rat cage whenever they visited with the 35 rats. Then Roland and Samuel would get loose. Under the bed, in the closet, behind the sofa—they were always finding a new place to hide (and leave pellet-sized reminders of their presence).

It didn't take long for me to grow weary of the rats in our house. They may have lasted one week—two at the most—before they were banished to the garage. They lived out there for another week before "it" happened—the boys left the lid off their cage again. Once more Roland and Samuel were at large in my home. Only this time they found a home where they thought we would never get them—inside the drywall of the house.

At first it was somewhat humorous. We would come out into the garage and see Roland and Samuel dashing back to their hole to avoid being apprehended.

But that got old fast. The day they dashed through my legs I thought I would have a heart attack. The garage wall where they had apparently taken up permanent residence began to smell like rats lived there—funny thing!—and the less-than-pleasant odor was drifting into my kitchen. So I finally confronted David. "Those rats have to go. Period. I don't care how you catch them, or where they go, but I want them out of my house."

Being a rather responsive man and also sensing that the rats were affecting my emotional state, David set out immediately to capture them. He apprehended one within days. The second (we'll call him Samuel) remained on the loose and managed to outwit virtually every attempt we made to catch him.

After a couple of weeks, it became apparent to me that David had lost his zest for catching Samuel. But I became more and more annoyed by Samuel's presence and especially by the thought that we had been outsmarted by a rat. So one morning when I arrived home from an early morning walk and found Samuel perched up on the seat of the golf cart, I determined to take matters into my own hands.

(You may be wondering why I didn't do that sooner if they were bothering me so much. If they had been called hamsters or gerbils, I might have considered it. But rats? The only thing that could move me was sheer desperation!)

I now put into action phase one of my plan, which called for blocking off the entrance to Samuel's hole in the wall. Since I just happened to be standing between him and the hole, that was a relatively simple thing to do.

"You will never go inside my wall again, you little rodent!" I

"Experience is valuable in most human endeavors, but the problem of getting a cat down out of a tree (or rat out of your garage) is new every time it arises."

Francis Duffy in
RoomMate Magazine

36

shook a finger at Samuel as he dived into the innards of our golf cart, another of his favorite haunts. That suited me just fine, as I had another important task to perform (phase two) that would seal his fate—closing the garage door. The door rumbled down, and that's when it was my turn to give Samuel the surprise of his little rodent life. I lifted up the cover of the golf cart motor, and there he was—exposed to the world (and me!).

Unfortunately, phase three of my plan was not yet developed.

Samuel had his own plan, however, and it involved getting out of view as quickly as possible. He dived for his hole in the wall, only to find it blocked off. He raced toward the usually gaping garage door, to be cut off. He scampered through my legs, and I screamed bloody murder, wondering what to do next. But Samuel was finally out of sight—under some shelving in the corner of the garage.

That's when phase three of the operation came into play. I began gathering junk from the garage (there was no shortage of that) and building a little fence around Samuel's hideout. Soon there was no exit, except into a waiting bug net I had commissioned for the occasion. But Samuel just wouldn't come out. I tried to push him out with a tennis racket. I tried to coax him out.

"Here, ratty, ratty, ratty."

I even ordered him out, but to no avail. That's when I remembered David, still basking under the covers in our bedroom—and went to recruit him. It was now just past 6:30 on a Sunday morning, and David was obviously pleased to be dragged from bed to participate in my rat-catching mission. He soon warmed to the occasion, however, and the chase began in earnest. In order to capture Samuel, we had to let him escape from his hideout. That's when the excitement really began. As soon as Samuel exited his hideout, I blocked that too. Then he had no place to go. He ran this way. He ran that way. I stood on the golf cart, screaming and wishing I had a video camera, while David, with his bathrobe and bug net, raced around in hot pursuit.

Then with one athletic swoop of the bug net (which just happened to land in the right place at the right time) Samuel was captured. Held aloft in the net, he looked just as surprised as we were.

Well, I have to admit, I was more than a little bit pleased with myself for initiating the chase, even though it was David who finally made the big catch.

"There is a time to let things happen and a time to make things happen."

Hugh Prather,
Notes on Love and Courage
[Doubleday]

37

It was one of those dreaded tasks that I could have put off forever were it not for the rhapsody of odors that kept drifting into my kitchen.

Caught a rat and proud of it,

Cari

FOUND IN MY FILES

"The longer I live, the more I realize the impact of attitude on life. Attitude, to me, is more important than facts. It is more important than the past, than education, than money, than circumstances, than failures, than successes, than what other people think or say or do. It is more important than appearance, giftedness, or skill. It will make or break a company . . . a church . . . a home. The remarkable thing is we have a choice every day regarding the attitude we will embrace for that day. We cannot change our past . . . we cannot change the fact that people will act in a certain way. We cannot change the inevitable. The only thing we can do is play on the one string we have, and that is our attitude. . . . I am convinced that life is 10 percent what happens to me and 90 percent how I react to it. And so it is with you. . . . We are in charge of our attitudes."

CHARLES SWINDOLL

REFLECTIONS

1. Is there a "runaway rat" near your kitchen (e.g. a dreaded task that you can and should really tackle, but have put off for too long)?

2. Assuming the unfinished task is really bothering you, why do you think you are delaying the task?

3. What can you do to get started and tackle the task once and for all (short of getting out the bug net and waking up some bleary-eyed accomplice at 6:30 a.m.)?

4. How do you think you would feel if you finished the task?

Chapter 8

SHARING YOUR TABLE

Dear Cari:

I laughed out loud when I read your runabout rodent story! I tried to imagine David's athletic swoop in his bathrobe! He's such a good sport! So hospitality isn't the order of the day for rodents in your house? That's OK; I can understand why.

But your letter did get me to thinking about hospitality and how, like many people, Roland and Samuel weren't wanting to be entertained. They needed safety and security, a place to be themselves.

We can find joy sharing our home with others, but each of us has to find a way that works for us. I remember hearing of a residence hall dean's wife who always left their door unlocked, and the boys were free to come in at any time to make sandwiches from supplies in their refrigerator. As much as I enjoy having students in my home, it needs to be at my invitation—or at least I need to answer the door. I could never be comfortable having people roam in and out of my house unexpectedly!

Actually, having people in our home has been a comfortable thing for me, something I have wanted to do. Although we didn't have lots of people in and out of our home on a daily basis when I was growing up, holidays were times when 20 to 30 family members all gathered for the day. My grandmother did lots of special cooking and decorating, which I thoroughly enjoyed. And so cooking for a crowd has been the order of the day for me.

I remember the first time I thought of the differences between entertaining and hospitality. It was in reading Karen Burton Mains' book *Open Heart, Open Home*. I recall a statement she made that God can awaken in us abilities that seem to have no relationship to our natural abilities, and that we need to learn to listen when God knocks at the door. She said our churches are filled with strangers and sojourners and that the homes and lives of our congregations are often closed to one another.

Don and I have found great joy in sharing our home with others. Oh, a few times it has been a snake, a bunny, a couple of

"When we exercise hospitality, it can be a way of saying thank You to God as well as a way of sharing His love with others."

Yvonne G. Baker

field mice, a stray cat or dog, a stray child or two, and I must admit I haven't always felt hospitable, but God has given me many opportunities to use His gifts in sharing our home. People are still my favorite visitors!

Once it was five teenagers! And Ryan was the one who first practiced the gift of hospitality. He came in one early evening and asked Don if there were any spare rooms in the residence hall. It was registration week at the college, so there were no spare rooms!

When Don responded and then asked why he was asking, Ryan said, "Well, there are some kids who don't have anywhere to stay tonight, and I just thought maybe they could stay here." When we told him it would be fine for him to bring these kids home, he said something like, "Well, these aren't like the regular kids you're used to."

What transpired next was a truly memorable evening. Ryan borrowed the car and sometime later came in the door with a teenage girl and four boys. They were beyond description. They looked like something out of a pop-culture magazine. Their hair, their clothes, their countenances were very different from the "regular" kids we were used to.

The story was that Ryan had met this young girl, and she called him after her stepfather had thrown her (literally) out of the house. She had these four other friends who were also alienated from their families. When they came in, they were uncommunicative, and I was at a loss at how to help them feel at home. When I asked if they would like something to eat, they all declined. However, Ryan told me that he knew the girl hadn't had anything to eat since the day before. I thought, *No one can resist my warm, homemade chocolate chip cookies*, and so I pulled out the ingredients and started baking. Once the cookies came out of the oven, they softened (the teenagers, that is) and tentatively ate a few. Eventually, they even ate some fried egg sandwiches. I remember vividly how the girl's hands just trembled as she put the sandwich to her mouth.

I wanted to reach out to these kids, but they seemed so unapproachable! Pretty soon the guys needed a smoke. Ryan had earlier informed them there was no smoking in our house. Actually, there's no smoking on campus! But he did escort them out to our backyard to smoke—we couldn't ask them to walk a mile (not even for a Camel)! I wondered how many people were

"If you live in a house full of teenagers, it is not necessary to ask for whom the bell tolls. It's not for you."

Bill Vaughan

40

looking down from the residence hall rooms to see cigarettes smoldering, blue smoke ascending. It got later and later, and I was so tired. I had to get to bed. I made up the hide-a-bed in the family room for the girl, gave her a nightgown, and showed her the bathroom. At first the boys refused anything—blankets, pillows, showers. But eventually we spread out blankets and sleeping bags in the living room for them, and they said they would sack out there.

Even though I was tired, it was hard to go to bed. I stood in our dining room and looked down into our living room with all the bedding and the boys sitting around on the sofas, and I said a little prayer. I said, "Lord, there's nothing in this house that I can't live without, even though some things are very precious to me. I will take whatever comes with the morning."

Well, day dawned. It was Ryan's first day of classes as a college freshman. I had to leave early, so he got breakfast for the five of them. He actually missed his first college class (he didn't trust them alone in our house either) to help them get on their way. He never heard from them again, but we have never forgotten those late night guests! It was our family value to use our home as a form of ministry. This experience stretched the limits of our commitment, and we had to put feelings aside and practice acceptance. We were proud of Ryan for his loving response to people in need.

I was also thinking that hospitality and food are linked so closely together!

These days I look forward to having people in our home for a meal, so we will sit down and enjoy a leisurely meal at the table. With our busy schedules, we now more often graze than sit down together to eat. I seem to find some comfort today in seeing similarities of my busy lifestyle in those around me. It seems we're all in the same boat.

Yet I find myself fondly remembering the days when the four of us regularly sat down and ate together at our table. I've thought of the summer afternoons and evenings when Don read a chapter after each meal, while we were still at the table, from the Five Little Peppers, Bobsey Twins, or Sam Campbell books. I wish we had done it longer, done it more! I thought of the Friday night candlelight suppers we had for years. But those days are gone except for when we have company. When the teen and college years crept up on us, we sat down to the table less, ate together less often. I'm not sure that was such a good idea. Even though

"A house without love may be a castle, or a palace, but it is not a home; love is the life of a true home."

John Lubbock

41

our table is still an important part of our home—and my heart is most full when many are seated around it on occasion—the daily opportunities to gather our little family around it are gone. And that reality makes me a bit sad.

We have several holiday traditions that are linked to being around our dining room table. Here's what we do at Thanksgiving:

On each person's plate, five kernels of dried corn are placed. After everyone is seated, Don begins by sharing that the kernels are placed there as a remembrance of the first Thanksgiving when the Pilgrims expressed their gratefulness to God after enduring their first hard winter. He invites each person to pick up one kernel of corn and express to the others how that represents one thing he or she is thankful for, and then the next person has a turn. Sharing continues until each person has had an opportunity to share five different times.

In the course of this we have had nodded heads, smiles, laughter, glistening eyes, tears, and even the response, "I'm thankful this is the last kernel of corn so that we can eat!"

I remember hearing of another family that does something similar with dried beans. However, they each place their beans in a small pot, and the next day these beans are soaked and then cooked in a soup made with leftover turkey and vegetables. They say it's the most delicious soup they've ever had.

I picked up *Advice for a Young Bride* at Ervin's Millwork Shop in Indiana just the other day. This is advice for the '90's woman of the Amish community. I was reminded that not everyone chooses to live the way we do. And I was touched by this advice. I'll send you a copy.

Well, I'm hungry; think I'll get something to eat. Anyone coming to your house for dinner (or any spare room in your garage)?

Sue

FROM MY FILES

YOUNG BRIDE

"As you set up your new home, young bride, you'll make many decisions and choices . . . furniture, paint, paper, curtains, and so on. May I suggest that you must choose wisely as you pick out one particular piece of furniture. A TABLE. This choice will affect the tempo of your life for years. First of all, make it sturdy above beautiful. It will need the strength when your garden pro-

"She has a dinner set that she likes a whole bunch, but we don't use it unless somebody important comes over . . . like my dad's mother."

Anita, age 9, from
My Mother Is the Best Gift I Ever Got,
by David Heller

42

duces a bountiful supply of beans and you and your mother sit down to snap those beans. It will groan under the weight of food as you feed your company.

"As your family grows, leaves home, and returns to visit, your table will need strength to hold babies and diaper bags, giggling toddlers in zippered snowsuits, and food to feed an ever-growing crew.

"The chairs that cluster around your table must also be strong, as your children grow into adult men and women. These chairs will need their strength as teenagers lean back and balance precariously, all laughing at the antics of a particular school day.

"Your chairs will need strength and comfort as your husband sinks wearily into them at the end of a long hard day at work.

"Make sure your table has a durable finish, one that will stand the water that soaks through a newspaper, a finish that will wipe up easily when your children reach too hastily for a glass of milk and send it careening over. The finish on your table will taste the salt of tears as you bandage cut fingers.

"Countless coffee stains will wipe away as your husband, neighbors, and salesmen have discussions about business.

"You may yearn to spend hours choosing sofas, curtains, painting, or accessories, but heed well my words about your kitchen table. Make it the hub of your family's life, and it will serve you well.

"When you are no longer young and radiant and you and your husband sit alone at your table's side, the memories you share will be joy, love, happiness, and peace in your aloneness. Choose well, young bride, choose well." (Erwin's Millwork Shop, Shipshewana, IN)

From *Open Heart, Open Home* by Karen Mains, here are some thoughts on what true hospitality is—and isn't.

✔ "Entertaining is

"Saying 'I want to impress you with my beautiful home, my clever decorating, my gourmet cooking.'

"Entertaining always puts things before people. 'As soon as I get the house finished, the living room decorated, my place settings complete, my housecleaning done—then I will start having people in.' 'The So-and-so's are coming. I must buy that new such-and-such before they come.'

"Entertaining subtly declares, 'This is mine—these rooms, these adornments. This is an expression of my personality. It is an

"Hospitality does not try to impress, but to serve."

Karen Burton Mains

43

extension of who and what I am. Look, please, and admire.'

"Entertaining looks for payment—the words, 'My, isn't she a remarkable hostess!' a return dinner invitation; a job advancement for self or spouse; esteem in the eyes of friends and neighbors.

"The model for entertaining is found in the slick pages of women's magazines with their appealing pictures of foods and rooms.

✔ "Hospitality is

"seeking to minister. It says, 'This home is not mine. It is truly a gift from my Master. I am His servant and I use it as He desires.' Hospitality does not try to impress, but to serve.

"putting people before things. 'We have no furniture; we'll eat on the floor.' 'The decorating may never get done. Please come just the same.' 'The house is a mess—but these people are friends. We never get to see them. Let's have this time together anyway.'

"putting away our pride, not caring if other people see our humanness. Because we are maintaining no false pretentions, people relax and feel that perhaps we can be friends.

"the idea that 'what is mine is yours.' This is the secret of community that is all but lost to the church of the twentieth century. 'And all who believed were together and had all things in common' (Acts 2:44, RSV). The hospitality of that first-century church clearly said, 'What is mine is yours.'

"doing everything with no thought of reward, but taking pleasure in the joy of giving, doing, loving, serving.

"The model for hospitality is found in the Word of God."

REFLECTIONS

1. How do you see your home being used as ministry?

2. Whom do you know who shows true hospitality? What do they do or say that communicates this?

3. What excuses or reasons do you find you give as reasons for not opening your home? What would you like to do differently?

4. Are the homes of your church open to one another? In your opinion, why or why not?

Chapter 9

ANGELIC CHURCH BEHAVIOR (AND OTHER HEAVENLY MYTHS)

Dear Sue:

Guess what? I actually had somebody asking *me* for advice. Seems this friend is having trouble making it through the church service. I have to admit that I have a few rather well-developed views on that matter! First, of course, I had to share with her my personal experience.

You know that saying "having one of those days"? Well, I've had plenty of "those days"—and they always seem to fall on the same day of the week (can you guess which one?). If I had to guess, I'd bet the person who wrote that song "O Day of Rest and Gladness" never had kids.

Here's my personal recipe for trouble—take three ear infections, mix with one sleepy husband, and stir in two squirming rascals. Let set for 30 minutes, then add one mom (bearer of the third ear infection) who's always late to church but never wants to be. Sprinkle in a late start, douse with hurried baths, a messy breakfast, showdowns over "yucky-tasting" antibiotics, and what do you have? A battle-worn mom with "that look" on her face.

It didn't take long for an observant friend to notice. "Looks like you're having a bad day," she whispered.

"Yeah—ear infections."

"Mine has one too." I got an understanding look.

Having survived the children's lesson study, we headed out for a snack and diaper change before church. It was then that David revealed a little "surprise"—it was Communion day.

I immediately envisioned long prayers, interrupted by squirms and squeals, finally brought to a halt by a late dismissal. I thought of a young man I knew who fasted before each Communion Service in order to prepare himself spiritually for the greatness of this event. Then I thought of my own frustration, exasperation, missed personal devotions, and lack of spiritual preparation.

"On a spiritual scale of one to 10, right now I'm about a minus 50," I whispered. "Just take me home."

"I'll watch the kids so that you can take part," David said.

"Doctors say that having a new baby in the home makes the days brighter. They should also include the nights."

O. A. Battista

45

"I'm in no shape for that. I'll probably just sit there and cry the whole time. Take me home." [Pause] "No, I'll stay."

The debate raged in my mind. Wasn't it a sin to take part if your heart wasn't right? *I don't even know why I came to church*, I thought. *I'm really a failure*. Then I remembered what the pastor had just said, the one snatch of his sermon I had been able to catch all morning—"Open to anyone."

Guess that means me, I thought. "OK, I'll stay."

When I got to the room with the other women, all I did was cry, and cry, and cry. The friend I took part with thought something must be dreadfully wrong and hugged me. It's hard to explain what happened to me during that Communion Service, but I actually felt better afterward. And I *was* glad I stayed.

I have had some "good church days," of course. One time we actually came up with something that kept my two preschoolers entertained the whole church service (as well as the children and adults in the pews around us). My husband had presented a nature nugget to a group of older children and just happened to have used a specimen of a bat in a clear glass jar. Although this was tucked away in the diaper bag, it was discovered and joyously held aloft by my children. Before I even realized what was happening, the older lady behind us was leaning over for a closer look, and the academy principal's three girls ahead of us were craning their necks to try to figure out what in the world we had.

Not wanting to seize the prize and make a scene, I instructed the boys to keep it low, and silently wondered what people must think of us when other children color and play quietly with felts at church and mine are observing a dead bat.

Today Michael and Matthew are older and things (for the moment) are better! But for four years (that's 208 weeks!) of my life I struggled with how to survive the 11 o'clock church service. Hearing the sermon was hardly an option. I was usually interrupted so many times that after about 5 or 10 minutes I completely lost the speaker's train of thought and never quite figured out what he was talking about again.

The most important thing I had to remember was that "this too shall pass." And sure enough, it has. Not without some major frustration on my part. I even told an aunt one time, and I meant it too, that I hated church and didn't give a rip if I ever went again.

I'm sure that there will be new challenges as my children get older, but for now some very tough days are behind me. And I'm

"One kind word can warm three winter months."

Japanese proverb

46

happy to say that a less-than-positive attitude on my part is also behind me. Church is once again a joyous experience (usually!). I can listen to a sermon from start to finish (with a few minor interruptions) and feel genuinely fed each week (most of the time). What a blessing!

Heard the sermon this week,

Cari

FROM MY PERSPECTIVE

Having received my share of stares from the saints, I now offer my (hopefully) valuable insights on surviving the entire church service:

✓ Encourage your church to start a "Pew Partners" program, in which concerned and caring individuals without little ones give parents a hand. B.K. (before kids) my husband and I always used to sit with some friends in the Kalamazoo church and help them entertain their small children. We thoroughly enjoyed it, and I know it was a help to our friends. If I had it to do over again, I would look for someone who had showed an interest in my children and ask if I could enlist their help.

✓ Ask yourself, "Is there something that might predispose my child to unacceptable church behavior?" In my case, I learned that I had a hearing-impaired child (which lends itself to hyperactivity and inattention) and a second child who was emulating his older brother's behavior. A set of hearing aids did wonders for our son Michael—and our family. Some children become extremely restless if they are used to eating at 11:30 and church doesn't get out until 12:30. A sippy cup with juice in it might just get you over the hump. (Cheerios cereal was OK for the mother's room, but they tended to make a mess, other children wanted them, and they definitely drew stares the one time—out of desperation—I tried them in the sanctuary!)

✓ Take something your child can play with quietly during church—perhaps a favorite toy, puzzle, or coloring book. At the moment, my children really enjoy a coloring book or nature book.

✓ Try to receive some spiritual nurture at other times of the week besides church service. This does not mean to skip church; it just means to supplement what you are receiving. Study with a friend, watch an uplifting video, or listen to an inspiring religious program.

"Remember, when your child has a tantrum, don't have one of your own."

Dr. J. Kuriansky

REFLECTIONS

1. Have there ever been times when you wondered why you went to church?

2. Have you ever been blessed by a service that, in your heart of hearts, you really had considered skipping?

3. If your children are challenging you during the church service, what new strategies do you think might be helpful?

4. When was the last time you were able to hear the majority of a sermon? If you are missing a lot because of the needs of your children, what can you do to supplement your spiritual diet outside of church?

"The only thing better than a sleeping baby is a sleeping mother."

Beth Wilson
Saavedra

Chapter 10

CRAWLING UNDER THE PEWS

Dear Cari:

I was touched by David's reaching out to you at church and encouraging you to take part in Communion. That was a tangible expression of his love for you and Matthew and Michael! I was also impressed that you accepted his offer and responded by staying, even though you weren't sure your "heart was right." And the Lord did bless you. By choosing to stay, your feelings followed your behavior. That's a truth I hold on to. There have been many times I haven't felt like doing something or being somewhere or responding in a certain way. But when I have made the positive decision, my feelings have changed to be more positive.

Your dilemma of getting something out of church with little ones brought back many memories for me. First of all, I remembered a time when we were visiting a large church, and Ryan squiggled out of my lap and onto the floor. Before I knew it, he was crawling under the pews in front of me. What was I to do? I wasn't even in a church where people knew us! Ultimately, we corralled him—much to his delight, but I quickly retreated to the mother's room for the rest of the service. And that certainly wasn't a place to listen either!

But keeping things in perspective, he eventually learned to stay in the pew, to behave appropriately in church, and now there are many Sabbaths when I yearn for the days of having a little one snuggling (or struggling) in my lap! Even though Don was in the same church as I was, he was generally tending to other people's kids and not with us for at least some of the church service. I remember experiencing a mixture of feelings—helplessness, some resentment, and yet guilt because I should be thankful I had a husband (and one who was in church). My expectations didn't match my reality, and that was reason for struggle sometimes.

I guess the bottom line is that it's important for each of us to find a way of doing things that work for us. Like you say, for some people, that means finding other times to really worship and experience a closeness with God and seeing church as a time to

> "Happy is the child . . . who sees mother and father rising early, or going aside regularly, to keep times with the Lord."
>
> Larry Christenson

focus on helping little ones learn about going to church.

What seems most important is to not lose God in the process of parenting our little ones (and older ones too). I'm reminded that when Mary and Joseph lost Jesus in the Temple, it took several days for them to find Him again!

That's how it is when we take our eyes off Him, when we don't take time for worship and prayer. It can take us several days to find Him again.

Years ago I copied down this thought: "When temporarily you have less control of your emotions, don't consider yourself less than a victorious Christian." That's been a good perspective for me to hold to.

Here's a little story for you: One night a mother and father checked on their daughter before going to bed. She had a serene look on her face as she slept, and they noticed one hand clutched around the forefinger of her other hand.

At breakfast the next morning they asked her why she was holding her finger that way. "Well, I repeat the twenty-third psalm before I go to sleep like you have taught me," she replied. "I keep saying it over and over again. The Lord is my shepherd. That's five words. I start counting with my little finger, and when I'm at "my" I'm at this finger. I like "my" the best. He's *my* shepherd."

So, dear friend, when you're feeling frazzled and finding it difficult to get your needs met at church or it's difficult to find time and energy for personal devotions, remember that you don't want to lose sight of Jesus. It might also help to repeat the twenty-third psalm when you go to bed!

Let's keep in touch,

Sue

"Let the heart of them rejoice that seek the Lord. Seek the Lord, and his strength; seek his face evermore"

(Ps. 105:3, 4).

P.S. My friend Alice recently shared this encouraging verse with me:

This year I am committed to being

    saved
    Spirit-filled
    seeking
    submissive to God's will
    suffering
    saying Thanks

REFLECTIONS

1. How comfortable are you in what your children are learning about a personal devotional life?

2. Some occasions when Jesus has given you "rest" have been . . .

3. A text that encourages you in your walk of faith is . . .

4. When you have less control over your emotions, do you tend to feel less like a victorious Christian? Where have you gotten this message? What can you do about this?

"Look around you and be distressed. Look within you and be depressed. Look to Jesus and be at rest."

Anonymous

"I Came Out!"

Dear Sue:

Thought you might like to hear about these deep conversations Michael and Matthew have been having lately. Kids have such innocent ways of capturing the real essence of a situation (and making the most of it). Sometimes they are a little off-target, as Michael has been recently. He's been struggling with a major issue in life—at least to his mind.

"Mommy, why am I bigger than Matthew?" he keeps asking. Matthew is two years younger, and there's no lack of competition between them.

"Well, you came out first, which makes you older," I keep telling him. "Because of that, you'll probably be bigger for a while—at least until you're grown up."

Having restated this explanation many times, I have been surprised that only one phrase of my lengthy explanation seems to stick in Michael's mind. "I came out *first!*" he keeps saying. After all, isn't being first a natural thing to be happy about? "I came out first, so I'm bigger." Or "I get to stay up later, play with this toy, or have something I want—because I came out first." This line of reasoning became old rather quickly. However, despite repeated attempts at attitude adjustment on my behalf, Michael continued to use it.

But today Matthew invented his own little comeback that seems to successfully end each tiff. Whenever confronted with the "I came out first" theory of evolution, Matthew just jumps up on something (to make the most of any available height advantage), squares his little shoulders, looks down on his brother, and pompously declares, "I came out!"

Of course, the truth of his statement was undeniable, and the end result is usually a draw. But something about Matthew's closing argument is sticking with me. "I came out." Whether first or last, rich or poor, red, yellow, black, or white—what really matters is that he is here.

I bet that's something you could share with the moms you

speak to or just about anybody. Whether you're energized, frazzled, pregnant, or in some other present state of existence, God loves you simply because you're His child. You may be a mother, but to God you're his sweet baby, to cradle in His arms of love and nurture oh so tenderly. You came out. You are His. And He loves you.

"I came out *too!*"

Cari

REFLECTIONS

1. Has your child asked you why someone is shorter, taller, bigger, or smaller than he or she is? How have you answered?

2. As you think about it now what do you think are the most important things for your child to hear when he or she asks questions about differences between people?

3. Has having children given you a new appreciation for what your parents (or other care-givers) might have felt for you as a child? Has it helped you to appreciate them more?

4. Some specific things you do to show each child he or she is unique and important to you are . . .

5. Some deep thoughts your children have expressed to you are . . .

6. In what ways do you see yourself as God's child? Why or why not?

"He who hesitates is bossed."

Anita Meyers

53

Chapter 12

TRUTH IS SHORTER THAN FICTION

> *"Our words should be like a magic canvas upon which a child cannot help but paint a positive picture of himself."*
>
> Haim Ginott

Dear Cari:

When I read your letter I was immediately reminded of how truthful children are with their statements. In their little ways, they share great truths! Your experience also reminded me of children's natural competitiveness with one another. Ryan used to tell Marci that he was in my tummy first (or they were in there together, I don't remember), and she was so big and fat that she squished him in the corner, so he shoved her out. In some way that made him feel more powerful.

Marci says, as a child, she was never sure that wasn't true, and it contributed to her feeling like she was too big and fat! I wish I could have protected them both from those feelings. All in all they were very companionable as they were growing up , but they have each sought ways to be assured of their place in this world!

It also makes me think about that complex issue of self-esteem. I believe it is Satan's goal to get us to question our significance to God and others, and that is something we will deal with until we go to heaven. It seems that Satan takes God's very best gifts to us and does all in his power to use them to hurt and destroy us. But we must remind ourselves that "We came out!" We are His. He loves us!

Long ago I decided that self-esteem isn't something we get and keep forever. It's a process of recognizing our potential and then living out that potential throughout our lives. One of the first people I heard talking about self-esteem was Verna Birkey. I don't know that she used the word, but I went to her seminar "God's Pattern for Successful Fulfilled Womanhood." It was very helpful to me personally as I was parenting young children.

I remember her saying that if we have grown up without the deep assurance of parental love, our mind has been programmed to receive such thoughts as "No one loves me" and "God doesn't love me." She explained that with God's help we can reprogram our mind according to facts and establish new thoughts. She cautioned that this takes conscious and diligent effort, but with

54

God's strength we can do it. I was more determined than ever that my children would grow up perceiving my love for them.

She said that our love toward our children should contain the same qualities that God's love has for us. She identified these qualities and gave us texts to support them:

Unending	Jeremiah 31:3; John 13:11
Unselfish	John 15:13
Unconditional	John 3:16
Undeserved	Romans 5:8
Unaffected	Romans 8:35, 38, 39

These days, almost every magazine has an article on self-esteem. An advantage is that now we are developing a better understanding of what self-esteem is and that we need it! I don't think we can take a "cookbook" approach to developing self-esteem in ourselves or our children. However, I am convinced that we need to realize our own worth in God's eyes in order for us to pass on worth to our children.

Actually the person who has had the most impact on my understanding of developing a positive sense of self-esteem, has been Jean Illsley Clarke. Jean has become a dear friend and mentor to me. She is very clear that positive self-esteem is not to be confused with self-centeredness or acting superior. Also, she suggests that some things in life we have control over, and other things we do not.

For example, we cannot control when or where we were born, the family we were born into, our sex, our race, our birth order, our overall physical appearance, or our basic personality. It's important to accept that these aspects of our life contribute to our sense of who we are. But to some degree we *can* control how we relate to the positive and negative things life offers. These also affect how we feel about ourselves. As we get older, we have opportunities to place ourselves in environments that provide us with interactions with others who see us as lovable and capable, and we can remove ourselves from negative environments and negative ways of thinking. Also, we can choose to see ourselves as lovable and capable, affirm ourselves—not always waiting for someone else to give us those messages.

The bottom line is that we have the God-given ability to choose what is helpful to us from both positive and negative experiences in life. I think it is a life-encompassing challenge to achieve a healthy sense of self-esteem in ourselves and to contribute to the

"Love talked about can be easily turned aside, but love demonstrated is irresistible."

W. Stanley Mooneyham, *Come Walk the World* [Word Books]

healthy self-esteem of others. Jean shares that "becoming contented and well-adjusted is a process filled with hope and is as important for us as it is for our children" (*Growing Up Again*, p. 8).

Jean says: "Self-esteem is a family affair. Because the family is the first place where we decide who we are and observe and practice how to be that way" (*A Family Affair*, p. 4). It is in our family that we get our first very important messages about belonging and where we get messages about what we can do well and who we can become.

I believe it's terribly important that our children learn that their belonging doesn't hinge on their behavior, that we learn to communicate love to them in ways that have meaning for them, and that we provide them with rules and structure that guide but don't shame or imprison them. They need to know that whether they came out first, second, last, or somewhere in the middle. They came out—and that's most important!

For my own sense of well-being, from time to time I need to go back to Scripture and read Psalm 139—to be reminded that I am "fearfully and wonderfully made" (verse 14).

Thanks for sharing words of wisdom from your boys!

Sue

P.S. I'm glad you were born!

"The one who loves me best, loves me most."

Quoted by Rose Otis at a Christian women's retreat

FROM MY FILES

One of my students wrote this poem while taking a class I taught on developing self-esteem:

"ON SELF-ESTEEM"
by Shirley Blake
"I have come
to this place
to this moment
as I
clearly a significant
individual. I
and within
am I
finding much love
magnificent potential
His legacy
is I
God's greatest gift to me."

God Loves Me: A New Thought Pattern
(Verna Birkey, Enriched Living Workshops)

1. *Meditate on God's love.* Memorize and meditate on biblical passages and verses that say or imply God loves you. John 14:1-6; John 13:1; John 15:9-17; John 17:20-26; 1 John 3:1-3, 16; 1 John 4:7-11; Jeremiah 31:3; Romans 8:28, 29.

2. *List people who love you.* Make a list of the people who have verbally expressed love and those who have done things that imply they love you. Write specifically the expressions of love they have given in words and deeds.

3. *Review at night.* Just before going to sleep, let your thoughts review the love God has for you by quoting and meditating on the scripture(s) you have learned. Then pray, thanking God for His love to you. Recall people who love you and thank God for them. Let this thankfulness be your last thought before dropping off to sleep. Establish this as a pattern. Practice it diligently for the first three or four weeks in particular.

4. *Rehearse in the morning.* In your waking moments when you may be tempted to revert to the old ways of thinking, rehearse these solid facts that God loves you and that people love you. Again, stop and thank God for the facts, disregarding the contrary feelings that are built on the old thought patterns.

5. *Share.* Share with others in detail what God's love means to you—as it becomes more real to you through your meditation on His Word, as you observe His love manifested in little evidences in your daily life, and as you see it manifested through the people He brings across your pathway.

6. *Sing.* Sing songs of God's love. Sing heart-response songs to Him like "My Jesus, I Love Thee" and "O, Love That Will Not Let Me Go."

REFLECTIONS

1. Some positive messages you received as a child are . . .
2. Some negative messages you received as a child are . . .
3. These messages affected your self-esteem in these ways . . .
4. A positive message you want to give your child is . . .
5. Something you want to do to build your child's self-esteem is . . . You will begin by . . .

Chapter 13

"Don't Tell Me That Ain't No Blue Jay!"

Dear Sue:

"I like the old me, but I'd love to have a new you."

Ashleigh Brilliant

Thought you might like to hear a B.K. (before kids) story out of me—although it does have to do with kids.

"Once upon a time" David and I, along with another couple, escaped for the weekend to what we thought would be a quiet campground by the lake. On Sunday morning the lake was scenic, the water quiet, and the four of us slipped into a canoe to see what we could see.

Unfortunately for us there were a couple of other lakeside visitors who had arrived on the scene for entirely different reasons than we had. For lack of a better term, let's just say there were two "bathing beauties" basking to the beat of their boom box in the middle of an otherwise quiet cove. From the looks of things, they had no apparent intention of moving anything but their mouths for at least five hours. And they were loud. Louder than their boom box.

Their raucous jokes and laughter seemed to reach us wherever we rowed on the lake. Whether we were "oohing" and "aahing" at a ruby-throated hummingbird or simply staring at a lily pad—their voices seemed always to be with us.

To make a short story even shorter, another lakeside visitor had also noticed the rather boisterous behavior of the two young ladies in question. Feeling somewhat annoyed by it all, he decided to vacate his sunning spot.

The camp visitor of whom I speak just happened to be a great blue heron, and his flight path toward a speedy exit posed just one problem: the girls were directly under it.

Being a rather fearless flier, and having determined to escape the area ASAP regardless of the consequences, he took off anyway. Our friends the ladies, having just reached a very temporary lull in their otherwise scintillating conversation, had just settled down on their backsides for a long, sunny nap.

Now, having never experienced the sensation of a great blue heron flying directly over my head, I can't tell you exactly how I would have reacted. But one thing seems fairly certain—thanks to the educational influence of my naturalist husband—I would have known what he was!

To this day when David and I see a great blue heron, complete with six-foot wingspan and crook-in-the-neck, we often look knowingly at each other and quote that girl on the dock—although we could never say it the way she screamed it: "Don't tell me that ain't no blue jay!"

David and I nearly fell out of our canoe laughing! Without being judgmental, I do have to admit I felt sorry that those girls had such little appreciation for nature. Having come to enjoy and love the magnificence of a nearby heron, it was hard for us to fathom that they couldn't recognize one from five feet away (although I suppose the one girl should be awarded partial credit for the rather astute observation that the big bird was not, by any stretch of the imagination, a blue jay).

I guess we were both right—he was a heron and he "ain't no blue jay!" Maybe it's all in how you look at it. What do you think?

Cari

REFLECTIONS

1. Give an example of a time when someone saw a situation differently from you. What happened?

2. What distractions may keep you from seeing things as they really are?

3. Are you taking time to seek new experiences by yourself, with your family, your friends? Why or why not?

"You can't always go by expert opinion. A turkey, if you ask a turkey, should be stuffed with grasshoppers, grit, and worms."

Changing Times, the
Kiplinger Magazine

Chapter 14

BY "PERCEIVING"
WE BECOME CHANGED

Dear Cari:

> "One of
> the best
> ways to
> demonstrate
> God's love
> is to
> listen to
> people."
>
> Bruce Larsen

Well, I guess you can never know what kids (even big ones!) are going to say! Your little blue jay incident gave me some food for thought.

I could really relate to your desire to enjoy the quiet beauty of the lake and how you may have felt intruded upon by those who did not appreciate it in the way you did. Funny thing, that's what often happens as kids grow up. Given a choice between the quiet canoe ride or sunning with a boom box, lots of teens would choose the sunning routine—even if we raised them ourselves and gave them every opportunity to enjoy the quiet canoe thing.

But with our own, we can have hope that as they get older they'll revert to enjoying the beauty of the quiet and notice the heron and other glories of nature. And, of course, we hope they'll thank their lucky stars that they had parents like us who instilled these noble values in them when they were children!

I was also thinking that what we enjoy in an experience is not necessarily what someone else is looking for. When we see beauty or enjoy something, it's easy to assume that those in our families will too.

Actually, we make lots of assumptions about people we know well, like our husbands and children. But the reality is that unless mom is very intent on checking out perception, she doesn't really know what they are thinking or feeling.

I'm reminded of a story I heard from H. Stephen Glenn, an educator and psychologist. He tells about a little 5-year-old boy who needed to have his tonsils removed. Just before the scheduled surgery, his parents went away for the weekend and left him and their other child with some friends. While they were gone, this little boy decided to take out his own tonsils. He found a spring from the hobby horse and put it down his throat, twisting it in an attempt to remove his tonsils.

The person caring for him had to rush him to the emergency room in a nearby hospital to have the spring removed. Of course,

60

the mother was very upset when she returned. When she talked with him she said, "Putting that spring down your throat was a very silly thing to do, wasn't it, honey? See all the pain it caused you?"

The little boy said, "No, Mom, it wasn't silly."

His mom insisted, "It was a very silly thing to do."

And the boy insisted, "No, it wasn't silly, Mom."

Finally a little bell rang in his mother's head, and she realized she was assuming that her son's perceptions were the same as her own. She asked, "Honey, what does 'silly' mean to you?"

He answered, "Something that you laugh at, and this was nothing to laugh at, Mom. It really hurt my throat" (H. Stephen Glenn and Jane Nelsen, *Raising Self-Reliant Children in a Self-Indulgent World*, Pima Publishing and Communications).

I bet his mom is very intent about checking out perceptions more carefully now!

I believe that when we care for and respect one another, one of the greatest gifts we can give is to check out their perception. And everyone's perception is unique.

My mother-in-law worked for a physician whose patients sometimes became confused and frustrated. She had this saying on her desk: "I know you believe you understand what you think I said. But I am not sure you realize that what you heard is not what I meant." She told me that years ago, and I have always remembered it.

Our perceptions are really the key to our attitudes, motivation, and behavior. I well remember a student we knew who didn't perceive that his parents really loved him. Actually, he was the envy of some of the other guys, because in his senior year his parents bought him a car and arranged to have it parked near the boarding school where we taught so that he could use it on vacations.

This student was in trouble at school, and his parents were asked to come to the campus. I will never forget that Sunday afternoon. His mom and dad sat in our apartment as they talked to Don. His mom was tearful, his dad would have been (if he had known it was OK for him to cry), and they both were mystified at their son's behavior.

His mother said something like "I just don't understand Paul (not his real name); we love him so much, and we try to give him what we can. Why, we just got him a new car for his eighteenth birthday."

And his dad said something like "And we came all the way

"In the eye and attitudes of the parents and teachers who raise and educate them, children find mirrors through which they define themselves."

William Glasser

down here today to see what this is all about."

And I was recalling what Paul had said to me: "My parents don't really love me. They think they can buy me things, and everything will be OK." As they left that day, I watched them from my kitchen window as they got into their car. And I thought sadly, *If he doesn't feel like they love him, no matter how much they say they do, it really doesn't matter.* Paul's perception became his reality.

That incident really motivated me to love my children and others in ways that they could recognize and accept my love. And part of that is checking out their perceptions and their view of the world.

I think our children are often uncertain how to interpret their experiences until they explore them with us, and that's an important way of showing our love. Just recently I was in a store that was filled with imports from Ireland, Scotland, and England—and lots of things were expensive and breakable. A mother came in with a little girl about 4 and a toddler in a stroller. As they got to the back of the store, the little girl said, "Mommy, you said we weren't supposed to touch anything in this store." There was a little pause, and then she continued with real concern, "And *our feet* are touching the floor!" She was doing a perception check! As is so often with young children, she was an excellent recorder but not such a good interpreter!

One last thing. I like to think of children's minds being like sponges. They are interpreting the world as an exciting, colorful, safe place, or as a dull, boring, or even unsafe world. Much of their perception of the world is based on what we teach them.

Keep paddling!

Sue

P.S. I also want to say that I believe it's our privilege to share God's world with our children so that they can know the difference between Big Bird, a great blue heron, and a blue jay!

Keep paddling!

> *"Love will always find a way to be practical."*
>
> Joe White

FROM MY PERSPECTIVE

One of the most helpful books I've come across is H. Stephen Glenn and Jane Nelsen's *Raising Self-Reliant Children in a Self-Indulgent World.* They suggest that seven tools are essential for people to see themselves as successful, productive, capable human beings. There are three "perceptions" and four "skills" that they name "The Significant Seven."

They define a perception as "the conclusion we reach as a result of an experience after we have had time to reflect on that experience." A skill is simply something we know how to do.

The Significant Seven

1. *Strong perceptions of personal capabilities: "I am capable."*

2. *Strong perceptions of significance in primary relationships: "I contribute in meaningful ways and I am genuinely needed."*

3. *Strong perceptions of personal power or influence over life: "I can influence what happens to me."*

4. *Strong interpersonal skills. The ability to understand personal emotions, use that understanding to develop self-discipline and self-control, and learn from experience.*

5. *Strong interpersonal skills. The ability to work with others and develop friendships through communication, cooperation, negotiation, sharing, empathizing, and listening.*

6. *Strong systemic skills. The ability to respond to the limits and consequences of everyday life with responsibility, adaptability, flexibility, and integrity.*

7. *Strong judgmental skills. The ability to use wisdom and evaluate situations according to appropriate values.*

I think these three perceptions are so important! When children are with people who consider them—and treat them—as capable, they are much more likely to perceive themselves as capable. Even when they are very young, children want to do important jobs—at least up until the time when they begin perceiving themselves or how they do things as inadequate. I think the second perception is at the very core of our existence, that of being significant to others. The third perception, of having personal control, helps children know that their thoughts, choices, and actions actually affect the events and circumstances of their life. When these perceptions are in place, then children can develop the four skills Glenn and Nelson identified. I see a strong tie between these perceptions and our spiritual experience. If we can believe that God sees us as capable and significant and that we can have control in our lives, we can be open to His leading and trusting of His power in our lives.

63

What a legacy to give to our children—instilling in their thinking that they are capable, significant, and can influence what happens to them! And when we then teach them skills in these five areas, they can be competent, confident, responsible, fulfilled individuals!

FROM MY FILES

THE TODDLER'S CREED
anonymous

If I want it, it's mine.
If I give it to you and change my mind later, it's mine.
If I can take it away from you, it's mine.
If I had it a little while ago, it's mine.
If it's mine, it will never belong to anybody else, no matter what.
If we are building something together, all the pieces are mine.
If it looks just like mine, it is mine.

REFLECTIONS

1. Do you tend to assume that others see things the same way you do?

2. How often do you direct your children's behavior or assume the reasons for their behavior rather than checking out what they were thinking or trying to do?

3. Is there someone who has a perception of you that is not accurate? How does that make you feel? Is there something you can do about it?

Chapter 15

CONFESSIONS OF A "WORKING" MOTHER

Dear Sue:

"Do you work?" "Do you work?" "Do you work?" Seems like I've been asked that question a lot lately. Of course I work! Tell me about a stay-at-home mom who likes that question, and I'll tell you about a woman in denial.

But for some reason I've been having a hard time answering this question, . . . although I did get overcome with creativity the other day and wrote out a little skit to answer the question.

Census taker with "hoof-in-mouth" disease: "Do you work?"

Harried mother (in the process of trying to fix a remote control car): "What do you mean? Are all my parts in working condition? Last I knew they were. It's this car I can't get to go."

CT: "What I mean is, do you have a job?"

Mother: "I have 10 jobs. I'm a teacher, nurse, cook, counselor, chauffeur, lover, day-care specialist, homemaker, referee, and mother. I also fix remote control cars."

CT: "But are you gainfully employed?"

Mother: "Depends on what you mean by a gain. Oh, I see little gains every day. Changes in attitude, my children learning to do new things."

CT: "Lady, what I mean is, do you get a paycheck?"

Mother: "Oh, that! Not in cash, I don't. I have to barter. Mostly I get paid in slobbery kisses, quick pecks, and spontaneous hugs. But come to think of it, if my 3 year old finds a penny, he usually does bring it to me. . . ."

Being a mother. Working. They do seem like one and the same, don't they? Personally, I haven't worked outside the home much since I had children. So I can't talk about what it's like to get around early and send my children off to day care or come home at the end of a busy day, switch into high gear, and try to get everything done before the next day. But I can talk about working from home—for outside pay, that is. And unfortunately it's not everything it's cracked up to be. Simply put—sometimes it's just difficult to draw the line between housework and for-pay

> "There is no such thing as a nonworking mother."
>
> Hester Mundis,
> *Powermom*
> (Condon & Weed)

MTM-3

work. It's easier to do the for-tangible-pay work and let the housework and even time with the children slide. And therein lies a problem. Oh, I'm still a work-at-home mom. But I've learned something. Most of my work is done at night after the kids are in bed, or in the morning. Being a morning person, I started this letter at 5:30 a.m. With any luck at all, I'll have at least a few pages done before they get up. But working from home is a constant juggling act.

I'll never forget the time when I did some phone consulting for a posh financial firm in Detroit. B.K. (before kids) I had provided software support for a C.P.A. firm, and having developed a relationship with the software company, they asked me to provide some help over the phone to a potential customer who was trying to evaluate his needs. I can't remember the name of the man I worked with or his company, but I do remember the company personnel answered the phone and conducted everything in such an incredibly businesslike manner that I imagined they all must wear dark suits and expensive cologne, not to mention working in a glass-filled sky-rise office.

Then there was me. I used to wear business suits, but for purposes of this assignment I just worked at home, in my jeans, from the phone—often with 6-month-old Michael balanced on my hips. That worked fine—for a while. One day I was talking with this distinguished businessman on the phone, bouncing Michael on one hip as usual and going to some unusual lengths to keep him entertained, when Michael developed a sudden case of the hiccups. I tried everything to keep him away from the phone, but any way I arranged him his little hiccuping mouth was up rather close to the receiver. My cover was blown! The man now knew that I didn't work in a posh office and wear a business suit. I was a work-at-home mom. And what I discovered was, that even though he didn't seem as receptive to the idea as many I have met since then, I really didn't care. As a mother with small children, they are just part of my "package." Sometimes when I go out, I find child care for them, and sometimes I can't.

Then there was the time when I was doing the accounting for a local hospital on a contract basis. I desperately needed some paperwork that was at the hospital. Being dressed in jeans (my usual), I bundled up Matthew, who was less than a month old, and Michael, not yet 3, and drove the four miles to the hospital. By the time I got there, Matthew was asleep. Being unwilling to leave him in the car, I leaned him against one shoulder and explained to Michael that we would just "run in, grab some papers, and run right out." Unbeknownst to me, the hospital board was then in session, and they had some questions on the financial statements. Unfortunately, I just happened to walk by the room (with a window) in which they were seated. They promptly instructed the secretary to flag me down and ask if I could field their questions for just a few minutes. They didn't seem bothered by my dress or by the fact that I had a sleeping baby on one arm and a 2-year-old, who didn't understand, tugging at my jeans the whole time. But I was. It seemed like the ultimate collision of my two worlds.

Being a mother and having an outside career at the same time is definitely a juggling act. I would not pretend to be an expert, but I have learned some very difficult lessons (many of them the hard way). I put some of my thoughts down on the following page.

> Still "working,"
> ## *Cari*

FOUND IN MY FILES

HELP WANTED: Male/female to work double to triple shifts. NO holiday weekends off. Long-term commitment (18-year minimum). Must have unlimited physical and emotional stamina. No pay, but high potential for satisfaction.

"I tried to teach
   my child with blocks.
He gave me only
   puzzled looks.

"I tried to teach
   my child with words.
They passed him by,
   often unheard.

"Desperately
   I turned aside.
'How shall I teach
   this child?' I cried.

"They keep talking about fixed incomes. I wish they'd fix mine."

JoAnn Thomas in
Door County, WI
Advocate

67

"Into my hand
   he put the key.
'Come,' he said,
   'Play with me.'"
       —Anonymous

A MESSAGE FROM A TEACHER

"One hundred years from now
   it will not matter
What kind of car I drove,
What kind of house I lived in,
How much money I had
   in my bank account.
Nor what my clothes looked like.
But the world may be
   a little better
Because I was important
   in the life of a child."
       —Anonymous

FROM MY PERSPECTIVE

TIPS FOR WORK-AT-HOME MOMS

✓ If your work involves a great deal of concentration and your children are small, recognize that it will be difficult to get anything done with them around . . . and accept it. I've found it to be less stressful just to get up early, or work an hour or two after the children go to bed, or find some child care for a couple hours a day so that I can work without interruption.

✓ Try to keep things in perspective. Even if your family is really relying on the income you might make, your children are still a top priority in your life. When Michael was 6 years old, he innocently reminded me of this one day as I was pecking away on my computer keyboard. He came into my office and said, "Mommy, when I'm a big man you won't see me so much anymore." Tears came to my eyes, and I stopped working and played a game of baseball with him—something I might not be able to do very often 15 or 20 years from now.

✓ Avoid get-rich schemes and large investments. I have always done much better when I played it safe. The idea of residual income sounds nice, but very few people ever achieve it. As for multi-level companies, 90 percent of them go under during their first two years of business, leaving a bad taste in the mouths of a lot of people.

✓ If you are considering starting your own business, talk over your plans with your husband (if married) or someone else you can count on to share his or her true reaction to the idea. It's easy to get excited about something and lose objectivity. I know—I've been there.

✓ Try to maintain a balance between what you're worth and having a kind heart. Businesses you buy from charge you a fair price for their products or services. Why should you mark yours down below what it's worth? On the other hand there may be times when you genuinely want to help a friend, and he or she really does want to pay you for whatever you did but unfortunately just doesn't have the money. In that case, consider bartering. I've done tax returns for jars of honey, musical tapes, even haircuts for my family.

✓ If possible, find something to do that you really enjoy. It will be much easier to work and be positive about it, if you really like what you are doing. (That's why I'm writing instead of doing tax returns now—and believe me, it has made a major difference in my personal level of contentment, which incidentally, also affects my family.)

REFLECTIONS

1. What messages are you getting from others about your working, or not working?

2. How do you feel about these messages?

3. Something you're good at "juggling" is . . .

4. An insight you had from reading this chapter is . . .

Chapter 16

SANDWICHED IN TIME

Dear Cari:

How interesting you would be thinking about being a "working mom" just when I've been musing over my own "working mom" experience. Do I work? I'll answer that later.

Marci called the other evening. She said, "Mom, I've been thinking that you lived in a generation where you had to explain why you were working, and now I'm living in a generation where I have to explain why I'm not working—and I don't even have kids!"

So, Cari, I guess that makes you part of a sandwich generation—nestled between Marci's generation of focusing on professional fulfillment and mine when we were to find fulfillment in staying at home with our children.

Actually, I was a stay-at-home mom for several years and was really committed to that. I worked until the day Marci was born. Even though my boss did his best to convince me to continue working, I held my ground. Choosing not to work was kind of scary financially—and you wouldn't believe what we lived on in those days.

On the other hand, Don and I had made this decision together, and we were confident that God would bless our efforts to make it on one denominational salary. And we did for several years. However, having a responsible position as an administrative secretary one day and then coming home several days later to be there 24 hours a day with a new baby was an adjustment to be sure. But basically I knew in my heart this was right for our family. Oh, eventually I did work some here and there through those early parenting years—various typing jobs, substituting in the school cafeteria once in a while. My Avon route could be a story in itself!

Then when Marci was ready for first grade and Ryan for kindergarten, the home economics teacher resigned two weeks before school was to begin. The principal asked me to *please* consider teaching part time. What a struggle! There was a real need—it was the Lord's work. Was this His bidding? But what about my children? Don and I prayed and talked and decided to give it a try. I've been blessed to have a husband who has always been my encourager and has had confidence in my decisions. How we adjusted our household tasks (in a time when it was all woman's work) is another story.

Actually, harder for me than managing home and work was the attitude of some of our colleagues. I remember the morning when one of the teachers came into my classroom and in the course of our conversation said something like, "Well, we don't believe in a mother's working out of the home. My wife stays home and is making quilts to sell. Why she can sew at the machine for hours at a time and be right there with the kids!"

He had also shared the same "concern" with another friend who had also begun working part time, and she came to commiserate with me later that day. We both knew that at our houses we could be "home" but not be really "home" to our children. And we also knew what the kids could get into when we were at the sewing machine!

I found myself invigorated by interacting with the students and challenged by developing a curriculum. Yet I struggled with if I was doing the right thing. On one hand, I grew in many ways—and my children benefited from that—and yet looking back, that began a new era in our family, and I worked part-time throughout the rest of the children's growing-up years.

Sharing this with you brings to mind something Ryan told me—something that still pulls at my heart strings. When he was in college we were talking about memories of those days, and he told me that he remembers standing at the window and crying as he watched me go across campus every morning. I left about 15 minutes before he did for school.

He could have gone upstairs and stayed with our neighbors, with whom he was very close, but he was a "big boy" and insisted he wanted to stay home. He wasn't totally alone, though, because Don was there but was probably focusing on getting ready for the day. Neither of us realized that my leaving before Ryan did was stressful for him. Now, maybe he cried just once or a few times, but it's his memory, so it's his reality. And my reality is that I didn't know what was going on in my little boy's head (and heart), even though I was doing my best to be responsible to him and to my job. By the way, when he told me this, he reassured me that I hadn't

"I have given up some things to be a mom. But they are not gone from me forever."

Beth Wilson Saavedra

ruined him for life (some relief!).

I have to say that one of the true joys (or payoffs) of motherhood is to hear from the wisdom of your children. Of course, there are bits of wisdom from "wee ones." But in a conversation Marci and I had the other night, she also shared that she wonders if women of this generation aren't going to experience something similar to what men at retirement age are struggling with now. Many men have given their lives and souls to their work and don't have rich and fulfilling relationships with their families. She was reflecting that this will likely be even more difficult for women because of our deeper emotional needs for important relationships.

In her experience many of the working women she talks with aren't necessarily working for the common good of the family but for their own personal fulfillment. She wonders if they are looking outside for something that really can come only from within. She's met several hurt, searching, and depressed women, and rather than finding their value from within, they go to find satisfaction in their jobs. Yes, there is certainly appropriate satisfaction to be found in a job or profession, but so many women who need more nurturing, are not investing in relationships—with their friends, husbands, children—and I don't think we really know what all the consequences will be. On the one hand, we are privileged to live in a time where we have the freedom to work, but on the other hand, for many work does not bring true freedom!

Marci said she'd been thinking of the patients in a geriatric ward of a hospital where she worked several years ago. What really mattered most to those people was who was in their lives at the end. There's a bumper sticker that says "The person with the most toys wins." I don't think so. I'd make one that reads "The person with the most fulfilling relationships wins."

I think it's a hard call to balance work, a career, and parenting. The thing I do know is that children need and deserve adults who have the energy to care for their emotional and spiritual needs, as well as their physical needs. When you think about what it takes to succeed in the professional world for both men and women, it's quite a contrast to what it takes to meet children's needs. Think about it! To succeed in a chosen career, most people need to spend long hours, use their best energy at work, and be willing to move. But children need time together as a family, demand parents' energy, and need stability. At work adults can be efficient, assertive, and be high performers. With kids,

"And all thy children shall be taught of the Lord; and great shall be the peace of thy children"

(Isa. 54:13).

there's chaos (at least occasionally), so efficiency isn't always possible by any means, and sometimes there's no way of measuring what you've accomplished during any given day.

A few years ago a young couple we know had their first daughter, and they told us that they didn't know of any other couple (and they were part of a large church congregation and worked at a large hospital) who were choosing for the mother to stay home. The husband had taken his vacation time to be with his wife and new little daughter for two weeks. Friends and coworkers chided him for "wasting his vacation," and many were forecasting that after the usual six-weeks maternity leave, she would be so bored she would surely return to work. Well, she didn't. The down side was that they found no support for their decision and were questioning me if there was something wrong with them! I said, "I don't see how you can ever regret your decision. Blessings on you."

I do know this—now that my children are grown there are plenty of years for me to work full-time. For a mother to choose to stay home full-time or to work part-time or to work full-time is a decision she has to make for herself. It is not fair for any of us to pass judgment. But my heart tells me that if a mother can— and if she chooses to—stay home, she will likely never regret having done so.

Well, I must "get to work." I'm eager to know what you will confess to me next!

Sue

REFLECTIONS

1. Are you overworked or overcommitted? How does this make you feel? What can you do about it?

2. What are some qualities you bring to your "job"—parenting at home, work outside the home, etc.?

3. If you work out of the home, what does your child know about what you do?

"But seek ye first the kingdom of God, and his righteousness; and all these things shall be added unto you" (Matt. 6:33).

73

Chapter 17

THE CASE
OF THE HORRIBLE HORN RIMS

Dear Sue,

I lost a contact lens the other day, and it got me thinking about the evolution I've had in eyewear over the past 25 years. (Oh dear, do I sound dated?)

Remember the days of bell-bottom pants, platform shoes, and color-coordinated pantsuits with tunics that had to reach your fingertips? Or maxi dresses and rulers to measure the gap between skirts and knobby kneecaps? Or (one other prominent fashion note) when wire frames came in and cat-eyed glasses were out.

Unfortunately for me, at the tender age of 8, I was apparently stuck for life with a pair of appalling cat-eyes! Despite numerous bumps, breaks, and lens replacements, the hated cat-eyes lived on.

My parents seemed more concerned with providing food, clothing, and Christian education for us four kids than in making fashion statements. (I wonder why?) So, much to my chagrin, I was stuck—or so it seemed.

Then one day in Cheboygan, Michigan, my life was changed forever (well, not quite). Along with the rest of my Pathfinder Club, I waded into Black Lake for a cooling swim. In spite of strong feelings to the contrary, my swimwear included the conspicuous cat-eyes. I couldn't see without them. Several minutes and a few all-out water fights later, I decided I couldn't see much with them either. The lake was calm and shallow—its murky surface broken only by a nearby footstool-sized rock. Rather than wade into shore, I laid my glasses on the rock and continued swimming.

But when I returned about 45 minutes later to retrieve my spectacles, I was shocked to see that they had vanished! There were no waves on the lake, and they had been away from the water.

"You poor girl!" a nearby parent was quick to sympathize with me. "Here you are without your glasses." I was about to share her sentiments, when suddenly it hit me. The hated cat-eyes were gone! Forever! What seemed at first like a terrible misfortune (and was probably viewed in that light by my parents) turned out to be a blessing after all! It took all the self-restraint I could

"How often have we been too immersed in parenting to notice a shift in the emotional or physical landscapes of our children?"

Jonathon and
Wendy Lazear

muster to stifle a look of glee. After all, I had not lost them on purpose and did not want to make it look that way.

You know, I don't fault my parents for not getting me new glasses the minute cat-eyes went out of style. They did what they could to help me as I progressed from cat-eyes to plastic-octagons to wire-frame-octagons to contact lenses!

But it sure did mean a lot to me to wear something I felt really good about. So far everybody has been supportive of Michael's hearing aids, but I know that someday he might feel uncomfortable with them. And when that day comes, I want him to be able to get the kind that go inside his ear. They're not recommended for small children but will be just fine when he's older.

Oh well. I don't suppose you ever wore bell-bottoms, platform shoes, maxi dresses, or (perish the thought) cat-eyes.

Thankful for fashion eyewear—

Cari

P.S. I realize now that what I had always thought were horn rims were actually cat-eyes! Horn rims are evidently something men used to wear, but I thought the title fit my glasses just fine. The bottom line is that in my childish eyes both kinds of glasses were ugly!

REFLECTIONS

1. Something you wanted when you were growing up but that you didn't have was . . .

2. Something you felt self-conscious about as a child was . . . because . . .

3. Is this affecting you today? Why or why not?

4. Something I really liked to wear then that now seems awful was . . .

Chapter 18

CAT-EYES REVISITED

Dear Cari:

> "Every
> child is
> entitled to
> hold up
> his head,
> not in
> haughtiness
> and pride,
> but in
> confidence
> and
> security."
>
> James Dobson

Oh, the cat-eyed glasses! I had some too—black with silver on the top portion of the frames. I thought they were wonderful (if I had to wear glasses)—then! When I look at pictures now from that era, I'm all glasses!

I don't remember it being too painful to start wearing glasses. Mostly I remember how surprised I was, when I got mine in the sixth grade, to discover that I could see individual leaves on the trees and all the boxes on the shelves of the local pharmacy.

I had a friend in high school who, until she was about 13, didn't wear glasses. She played the piano beautifully, by ear, and her parents decided that she should also learn to play by sight. So they signed her up with a piano teacher and discovered she couldn't see the notes. All her life she had seen two of everything, as I understand it. Talk about perception!

I remember the day she explained it to me, wearing strange looking glasses that had double lenses for each eye. She said she knew she had two ears and she heard out of both of them, and she used both arms and both legs, so she just thought with two eyes, people saw two of everything. My heart aches as I've realized how hard she had to compensate all through her life. Also, it was very difficult for her to wear those strange glasses in high school!

When Ryan was in first grade, we had his eyes checked, and he was prescribed glasses. The frames weren't all that attractive. In fact, they weren't attractive at all! But it was all that was available for little guys then. Don and I were surprised at how upset we were that he was so nearsighted so young. Of course we knew it could be much worse, but that didn't lessen our distress much.

We said, "Why didn't we realize that two nearsighted people would likely produce even more nearsighted kids. Should we have not gotten married? Should we not have had children?" Now, I don't know if that's really true, about two people producing a child with even poorer vision, but it was quite painful for us to have our little guy in glasses so young.

Don and I both wore glasses, as did Marci by that time, so we thought the adjustment would be fairly easy—he'd be just like the rest of us (important for a 6-year-old, not so much for a 16-year-old). Interestingly, he lost them on the way to school very shortly after he got them. So off to the optometrist for another pair. Years later he admitted that he had "sort of lost them on purpose."

Two things come to my mind. One is the fact that we live in a nation consumed by focusing on beauty and intelligence and how that affects children's feelings of fitting in. And that contributes to the dilemma that your parents probably had—providing what their children needed without meeting all of fashion's demands.

I remember Marci and Ryan's singing of scripture verses to help them learn their memory texts. One that stands out in my mind was one of Ryan's memory verses—1 Samuel 16:7. Don usually worked with them in learning these scripture songs, but as I recall, they sang it as, "Man looketh on the outward appearance, but the Lord looketh on the heart. 1 Samuel, 1 Samuel 16:7" (KJV). I can hear that little melody in my mind as I write the words to you today—and it's been a few years! In the *Living Bible* it reads: "Don't judge by a man's face or height, for this [David's brother] is not the one. I don't make decisions the way you do! Men judge by outward appearance, but I look at a man's thoughts and intentions."

This is certainly an appropriate principle to teach our children and for us to live by ourselves. But the reality is that people's social needs are strong, and in our society appearance does have importance to people of all ages—including growing children trying to find their place in the world.

But we don't need to buy them everything! I truly believe that the best gifts for children are not things. I've seen parents try to placate their children by buying them things to keep them quiet in the store. But the greater needs of the child may be to get a good night's sleep, to be fed when hungry, and not to be expected to sit in the shopping cart for so long.

How to give our children what they really need is a tough one for most of us. Just the other day I was talking with a young mother of a preschooler. This single mom of two works at McDonalds' and has few resources. But in her own way she wants to do her best for her children. As the child surveyed the preschool classroom and headed for a large dollhouse, the mother said to me, "That's what I'm goin' to get her with my next pay-

"How quickly the patter of little feet turns into the padding of $150 Nike athletic shoes!"

check. She really liked a dollhouse at K-Mart. It's more than $100, but if she likes it, I'll get it for her!"

My inner reaction was *What? Spend that kind of money on a dollhouse for a 4-year-old, and you're on ADC?* Admittedly, my bias was showing, because of my own value system. Buying a child *any* toy for more than $100, *especially* when you are using government money, isn't what I would feel comfortable with. But the point is that she wanted to give her child what she thought other kids have.

And I do think we need to provide braces and glasses and becoming haircuts and appropriate clothing whenever possible. My experience has been that sometimes when parents don't provide these things, it isn't that they really cannot afford it, but it is because they don't see a need for it from their perspective. I remember hearing about a mother who insisted that her daughter wear her hair in braids because she thought the child looked cute in them. But no other children were wearing braided hair. I think her mother's insensitivity and insistence distanced her from her daughter. It added to the girl's feelings of not being understood by her mother, and it certainly didn't help the child fit into the social setting at school.

I certainly don't think we should remove every social challenge from our children. Appealing to your biological bent, I think of the trees in the rain forests as compared to those that grow in the desert. The trees in the forest are never forced to extend their roots downward in search of water, so they can be toppled fairly easily. But a tree planted in the desert can only survive if it sends its roots deep into the earth. We want our children to be deeply rooted so that they can withstand the storms of life and to believe that what God sees in their hearts is more important than what people may think from viewing outward appearances. Also, when it comes to the whys and why nots in our families regarding what we spend money on, what we do for entertainment, what types of clothing and accessories should be worn, I think it is important for us to explain *why* we do things that way. If I could do one thing differently, I think it would be to have explained the whys more and asked, "What is your understanding of why we . . . ?" or "What is your understanding of why we don't . . . ?" I often assumed that our children just "knew" why. Also, if we wait for our children to ask us, they probably won't. We will likely miss out on a lot of what they are thinking and wondering about. We need to create the time and place for open dialogue about our family's rules and values.

Along this line, I was thinking again about money. Families have lots of secrets when it comes to money! In our society most parents don't tell their children—or anyone else, for that matter—how much they make or what they have to spend. Too often children are told, "I can't afford that," when they ask for a certain kind of cereal in the grocery store. But then we go to a discount store and buy a new VCR or some cute clothing for the children. I'm acquainted with a family with five children where, when they were old enough, Dad involved the children in handling family finances. They knew how much money their parents had, helped write the checks, and made some of the decisions. Today these adult children are responsible with their money and are prospering. Having to turn off the lights to save money doesn't have much relevance to a child who doesn't have any idea how much money that could save; especially to someone who doesn't even understand how money works.

Thinking about the whys and why nots, family values, rules, and money reminds me that another thing we need to talk with our children about is stress. First of all, we need to learn how to handle our own stress. Then we can teach our children strategies for handling their stress. Life can be quite stressful—even for a baby! When we share with our children some of the stressors and social struggles we had when we were growing up, we can be such a resource to them. I firmly believe that we are our children's most important teachers.

Well, we horn-rimmed, cat-eyed people must get together soon!

Bye.
Sue

P.S. A garage may seem a strange place for inspirational messages, but this statement is hanging in ours, and I like it. When I drive in at night my headlights catch this saying: "Before you go to sleep, turn your problems over to God—He's going to be up all night!" It helps me handle stress.

FOUND IN MY FILES

Stress Issues for Different Age Groups by Dr. Archibald D. Hart
How do children of different age groups experience stress?   79

This depends partly on the child, of course, but certain stressors are predictable at different stages of development. Let me highlight some of the experiences and developmental issues that may contribute to the stress of each major age group. Note that these issues may include both causes and manifestations of stress.

Stress Issues for Preschoolers (Birth to Age 5)

- ✓ Discovery of autonomy and resistance to discipline
- ✓ Shyness and stranger anxiety
- ✓ Learning to share
- ✓ Learning bladder or bowel control
- ✓ Fear of the dark
- ✓ Separation anxiety
- ✓ Day care problems
- ✓ Destructive behaviors (hitting or biting)
- ✓ Temper tantrums

Stress Issues for Middle Childhood (Ages 5 through 7)

- ✓ Transition to school environment
- ✓ Heightened expectations for performance
- ✓ New competency issues: reading, writing, arithmetic
- ✓ Curtailment of physical activity—need to sit still
- ✓ Stubbornness and refusal to obey
- ✓ Jealousy over parents' love and attention
- ✓ Self-criticism
- ✓ Increased self-consciousness
- ✓ Excessive boasting to boost self-esteem
- ✓ Heightened interest in sexual matters
- ✓ Difficulty in handling rejection or failure

Stress Issues for Later Childhood (Ages 8 to 10)

- ✓ Moodiness, sulking
- ✓ Acute body awareness—demand for privacy, modesty when dressing
- ✓ Over anger
- ✓ Increased self-criticism and self-rejection
- ✓ Resentment of parental authority
- ✓ Growing sense of independence and autonomy
- ✓ Beginning of some rebelliousness, lying
- ✓ Deepening of school curriculum; higher academic expectations
- ✓ Exposure to drugs and substance-abuse issues
- ✓ Popularity, formation of cliques

✓ Heightened sense of competition—who can and can't, has and has not

✓ Concern over athletic success—performance and body image

For more information about older age groups and an in-depth look at how stress affects children and what parents can do, we suggest you consider the book, *Stress and Your Child* by Dr. Archibald D. Hart (Word Publishing).

THE BATTLE OF THE BULGE

Dear Sue:

It's amazing how what's important to my kids seems like more of a detriment to me! For example, since Matthew is the smallest kid on the corner, to him size is incredibly important. As far as he's concerned, the bigger the better, and he can't wait to be bigger.

This may help explain the bit of truth he so pompously shared with our neighbor boy the other day. They were sitting on my front steps, in the midst of a rather earnest discussion on such important topics as who was bigger, older, and could push the other one down. Having come out the loser on nearly every score, Matthew finally topped his friend by proudly proclaiming a fact that was beyond dispute, "My mommy's bigger than your mommy!"

Now, to Matthew being bigger is a very positive thing—important enough to inform his then-known-world about. Unfortunately, I can't say I shared his enthusiasm. To put it bluntly, I did not want to be bigger than the neighbor lady or any other woman who stands four inches taller than I!

My sons have made a few other astute observations about my figure (or lack of one) in their childish innocence.

"Mommy, your legs are squishy," Matthew chirped one day in his cheery little voice. Now, I never claimed to have the legs of a model, even in high school, but if I were to pick a word to describe their condition at that moment, "squishy" would probably not have ranked very high on my list.

Michael was a little more discreet. "Mommy, you're getting skinnier already!" he announced, just as I finished the first workout of a new exercise program. If only results happened that fast!

Personally, I've tried to address some of the emotional pain that accompanies my extra baggage with a dose of good humor. One of David's students shared with him her mother's favorite quip about weight gain: "I still have the same hourglass figure I always did," she confided to her daughter. "It's just that the sands have shifted a little bit."

To my way of thinking, that woman can count herself fortunate

"The end doesn't always justify the jeans."

Dorothea Kent in
The Saturday Evening Post

whose sands have only shifted, instead of shifted *and* multiplied!

Then there's a song that I've enjoyed singing during the past few years, although I'm not sure if I have the words just right. The song is entitled "Let There Be a Little Kindness," and the particular verse I am thinking of talks about more of others and less of me. I think the song is talking about unselfishness, but it seems to fit in some other instances, too!

I didn't always have a weight problem—not until I neared the big 30. To make a short story even shorter, I became pregnant with Matthew immediately after I had experienced a miscarriage, and my body didn't like it. So despite the fact that I couldn't even walk by the refrigerator without gagging during the first three months of that pregnancy, I somehow managed to gain 60 pounds anyway. I'm sure I did my share of eating during the last six months of pregnancy, but 60 pounds worth? That's a lot of donuts, and I didn't eat 'em!

But what matters not, at this moment, is how those pounds got there but how I have to get them off. I can't say I have been a smashing success, but I have learned a few things through my failures. Not that you need my insights, but I was hoping that somebody would!

Principle #1—Don't take yourself too seriously. When you have 60 extra pounds, they're not going to come off overnight. If there has been one lesson I have learned the hard way, it's that quick weight loss plans are about as effective as get-rich-quick plans. (In other words, they don't work.) And the faster you lose it, the faster you will likely put it back on. (I know—I tried!) In my book—and from the experience of countless others—the only way to long-term, successful weight loss is a lifestyle change.

Principle #2—Take a hike! (A walk will do, too.) Walking is a great form of exercise—one of the best, in fact. I try to walk 4-6 times a week. If you get tired of just walking, you can always try speed-walking, which burns calories even faster. Or water-walking, which is said to burn calories four times faster than a leisurely stroll down the street. But if you're not into either of these and think you would break your neck doing in-line skating, there's always slow walking, which is a whale of a lot better than no walking. And if you just can't seem to get yourself off square one, you can always "let your fingers do the walking" (through the yellow pages) so that you can implement . . .

Principle #3—Join a support group, or write in a journal.   83

"*Don't fight a good breakfast. Go with the grain.*"
Graffiti

It doesn't have to be formal. But you need someone you can talk to or a notebook to write on. And if you're married to a perpetually trim person, as I am, he's not the one! If you don't have a friend or friends, you can find some in a support group.

Principle #4—Light suppers are best. I just eat fruit for my third meal of the day—most of the time. In a study I read about, when two groups of people were fed the same amount of calories per day—with one group eating twice a day and one three times a day—the group who skipped the third meal either lost weight or gained less weight than the other group! But I understand that another study seemed to support the idea that four or five small meals during the course of a day helped people lose weight. For me supper is the most dangerous time of the day to eat. It's so easy to eat for emotional reasons. I'm tired and the kids are whining. My willpower is at its weakest, and food looks at its best!

I'll have to admit it. The first day I ate only fruit for supper I thought I was going to die! But I got used to it after a couple of days. And the results are starting to become obvious. This adjustment to my lifestyle has increased my willpower regarding eating, and it has also spread to other areas of victory in my life, including my spiritual willpower.

I do eat heavier suppers on occasion, such as when we are invited out. But this new way of limiting my suppers to fruit has helped me avoid a persecution complex, which in the past has led to eating binges. I have freedom to eat; it's just that I eat fruit for supper.

Principle #5—Stay away from fad diets. Those diets that say you can eat anything you want, where you want, how you want, and when you want are a bunch of fat-laden, deep-fried baloney. Having tried a few of them, I can speak from experience. Three-week torture programs only lead to binges—and more weight gain for me As far as I'm concerned the very word "diet" is dangerous. It's as though every meal is a battlefield when I feel that I'm being regimented on a diet!

Principle #6—Go low on the fats! There are a lot of hidden fat grams in foods, and I've learned to look at the labels. But there's one other important item to look for on the label: calories. A food may be low in fat and still be high in calories.

Well, I wish I could say that my lifestyle change has been so wildly effective that I'm now in danger of blowing away, but that isn't the case. But I've accepted that it will take time to do it

"If we can ever make red tape nutritional, we can feed the world."

Robert M.
Schaeberle in
*Management
Accounting*

right. And I feel and sleep better with the light suppers. That alone means a lot to me.

Cari

FROM MY PERSPECTIVE

THE EIGHT RULES OF DIETING
(which I hope no one will take seriously!)

1. If you eat something and no one sees you eat it, it has no calories.

2. If you drink a diet soda with a candy bar, the calories in the candy bar are canceled out by the diet soda.

3. When you eat with someone else, calories don't count if you don't eat more than they do. (The trick is to dine with a big eater!)

4. Food used for medicinal purposes *never* counts, such as hot chocolate, toast, and Sara Lee cheesecake.

5. If you fatten up everyone else around you, then you look thinner.

6. Cookie pieces contain no calories. The process of breaking the cookie causes calorie leakage.

7. Things licked off knives and spoons have no calories if you are in the process of preparing something. Examples are peanut butter on a knife making a sandwich and ice cream on a spoon making a sundae.

8. Foods that have the same color have the same number of calories. Examples are spinach and pistachio ice cream, mushrooms and white chocolate. NOTE: chocolate is a universal color and may be substituted for any other food color.

PANTRY POWER

"I can do it,
   I'll hop to it
   I have done it in the past,
"I can diet
   (If I try it)
   And those pounds will drop off, fast!
"I'll achieve it!
   I believe it!
   Dietary victory—
"Soon this little
   Pudgy middle

85

Will be ancient history.
"Diet fare—it's
　　Yummy carrots,
　　Goodbye chocolate! Hello greens!
"Drink some water!
　　Skip the butter!
　　Have some salad! Pass the beans . . .
"Don't conceal fat—
　　Exercise that
　　Paltry poundage off your waist!
"Wear a smile
　　and walk a mile!
　　Sit up! And fat will be erased!

—Cari Haus

REFLECTIONS

1. A "compliment" one of your children gave you once was . . . This made you feel . . .

2. Do you desire to gain or lose weight? Why or why not?

3. If so, what is keeping you from accomplishing this?

4. In reference to eating, is there something you want to do differently? If so, what? When will you begin?

Chapter 20

A Truly "Heavy" Issue

Dear Cari:

Thanks for sharing your battle of the bulge. Aren't kids charming?

Take comfort. If God hadn't loved calories, He wouldn't have made so many! All kidding aside, this thing about weight is a heavy item for so many of us. And for the people who aren't struggling with more weight than they want, they seem to be struggling to put on weight!

What comes to my mind is the importance of balance in our lives. We need to recognize the importance of being comfortable enough with who we are and how we look balanced with not acting like "denial is a river in Egypt" and refusing to come to grips with our physical appearance and health.

I was thinking about some of the messages we give to our children about food. Some messages are manipulative and induce guilt.

"What? You're not eating that? Why, think of all the starving children in Africa who would be thankful for what you have!" "Your brother is such a good eater; see how he's cleaned up his plate?" Or they pressure a child into a certain behavior or use food as a reward. "If you're good at the store today, we'll stop for ice cream." "You're going to sit here until you finish that food, and if it takes until tomorrow morning, too bad!" "Here, have a cookie, you'll feel better." These are the ways we teach our children to use food as a comforter. And certainly messages like, "No dessert unless you clean up your plate" or "You'll never grow up to be strong and tall if you don't eat . . ." can encourage overeating.

We can also send messages of disapproval, and our children may develop an unhealthy self-consciousness about their bodies with comments like "What? You want to eat again?" "You'll get fat if you eat all that chocolate!" "Those pants are getting a bit tight; . . . better cut down on the french fries."

So we learn young that food serves more purposes than just providing energy and nourishment for our bodies. I have a real sense of concern when I see adults putting a bottle in a baby's

> "Only a fool argues with a skunk, a mule, or the cook."
>
> Harry Oliver in Thousand Palms, Calif. *Desert Rat Scrap Book*

mouth at his or her first signs of distress. It's no wonder so many of us grow up using food as a pacifier—we had lots of chances to develop the habit!

And then as our children grow, they are vulnerable to the messages in the media and what they learn from our culture. There's a poster I've seen: "You can never be too thin or too rich." What a loaded (and dangerous) message!

I was also reflecting on the thought that we don't want meals to become a control issue. In reading *Meditations for Parents Who Do Too Much*, by Jonathon and Wendy Lazear, I came across this insight: "Oh, but the myriad of ways we use to cook broccoli! Chop it up and place it in the hamburger (they'll never suspect); process it into a fine paste and spread it on crackers; boil it into a delicious soup. We've got to get those kids to eat their broccoli.

"Do we? Will they grow up into unruly, unfeeling, unsatisfied adults if they never eat broccoli?

"Parents who do too much often act like slaves in the kitchen, trapped by their belief that kids 'need' certain foods, even if they don't want them. In fact, sometimes it's the foods they don't want that become an issue. We wage war in the kitchen, armed with our pots and pans, ready to do battle" (Meditation for August 4).

On the other hand, serving our children nutritious meals at routine times is very important. Eating together is also an important aspect of building a strong family. And introducing our children to nutritious food at a young age and teaching them how to select and prepare it are all part of the parent package. Research didn't make it true, but research does document that children who have regular, nutritious meals—including breakfast—perform better at school. Not only are they better able to concentrate on their studies, but also they are more in control of their behavior. It's really not fair to send children off for the day with anything other than the best we can do for them!

Well, so much for talk about food. I like it. I eat too much of it. God isn't finished with me yet!

Sue

> "A body is forsaken when it becomes a source of pain and humiliation instead of pleasure and pride."
>
> Shirley Billigmeier

FROM MY PERSPECTIVE

Many kids aren't learning about the benefits of a healthful diet at home. Kraft General Foods sponsored a survey of children.

It showed that one quarter of America's school children don't eat fruits or vegetables each day and that half of the children think apple juice has more fat than whole milk!

Parents are their children's most important teachers when it comes to healthful eating. Try the five-a-day plan. Provide at least five servings of fruits and vegetables each day. As children get older they can help keep track of the fruits and vegetables they eat. They can also help shop for fruits and vegetables, learning how to choose good quality fresh foods as well as selecting canned and frozen foods.

Remember that children do have food jags. It's normal. If children are offered a variety of nutritious foods, they will generally (within the week) eat a variety of foods to meet their nutritional needs.

Children's appetites usually decrease dramatically when they are about 1 year old, when their growth slows. Try serving about one tablespoon of food for each year of their age.

Don't assume that because children didn't like something last week that they won't like it now. Try it again!

Resist labeling your children by telling them or others that they are "picky eaters" or saying "They don't like gravy, can you imagine?"

Resist using food as a reward for certain behavior or taking food away as punishment. Using food as a tranquilizer or pacifier is not helpful to children. Punishing children by making them eat yesterday's uneaten food, for example, is not helpful either. It builds resentment and makes power and appetite a greater focus than healthful living.

Don't try to *make* children eat. It won't work anyway! In the long run, the power struggles are more detrimental than the nutrients missed at a given meal. Instead, let your children do their own thinking and feeling. It's OK if they don't like a particular food, but they need to learn how to balance what they like with what's healthful eating and appropriate manners.

Teach your children to care for their bodies by eating responsibly. Involve children in menu planning, shopping, and preparing foods. They tend to enjoy what they have had a part in choosing and preparing.

Study about nutrition yourself. Seek to understand how your moods affect your food preferences and how your food choices can alter your moods! Make meal times enjoyable, relaxing fam-

"A food is not necessarily essential just because your child hates it."

Katherine Whitehorn

ily times. Sit down and eat together as often as possible. If you don't establish that habit when children are young, they will likely resist if you surprise them with a "We're going to sit down and eat as a family tonight." Schedule eating together on your family calendar if necessary.

Read labels and teach your children to read labels.

Provide your family with lots of "yes" foods they can eat when they are hungry—fruits, vegetables, healthful crackers, and grain products.

Remember that the behavior your children see you modeling (the eating habits they observe in you) is more effective than all the instructing and preaching you might do!

Guide children in making lots of choices, and help them understand the results of these choices. For example, if children overeat and then find themselves with a bloated or queasy stomach, help them explore why they may be feeling that way and what they would like to do next time. If they choose not to eat, help them explore how it feels to be hungry and what they can do to be more comfortable until it is time to eat again. This needs to be done without shame and blame!

Remember, the more your children learn about nutrition and a healthful lifestyle, the easier positive choices should be as they mature.

Guide them in making lots of choices, and help them understand the results of their choices.

REFLECTIONS

1. Some messages you got about eating and food when you were growing up were . . .

2. What are you teaching your children about eating and food?

3. Do you eat when you're not hungry? Why or why not?

4. Reflect on 2 Samuel 22:33: "God is my strong fortress; He has made me safe" (TLB). In what ways is God supplying your basic needs of food, shelter, and safety?

Chapter 21

A SONG IN OUR HOME

Dear Sue:

I just had a burden to share with you one of my parenting experiences that, frankly, isn't very funny. We've talked a little about expectations or surprises—and sometimes in a humorous way.

One of my biggest and least pleasant surprises as a parent came three years ago. My son Michael, who was 4 at the time, did not seem to be hearing us as well as we thought he should. In addition, his speech seemed rather unclear. I had a gut feeling of concern about this for a year, but whenever I mentioned it to others, they would say, "Oh, a lot of children don't speak very clearly at that age. They all develop differently."

What was strange, however, was that I remembered Michael speaking more clearly a few years before. I looked at his hospital chart for when he had pneumonia at the age of 2, and it said "clear speech," "wide vocabulary for his age," and things like that.

One other thing I just could not figure out was why Michael did not like to sing anymore. He was always my singer—up until the time of that one 48-hour hospitalization. A friend who provided us some child care during that time said, "My, he is always singing!"

And I will never forget in camp meeting one time—standing in a huge auditorium with thousands of people. Michael was our little "Gerber baby"—1 year old, bald as could be, and (we thought) cute as a button. We were singing a hymn, and Michael got inspired to sing too. He was perched up between us behind the hymnbook, our only little one at the time, and he sang on one note rather enthusiastically during the whole song! He had his mouth wide open and such a sweet innocent look! I can still remember thinking *He's our little choir boy!* And I cherished the amused but approving looks that people around us gave.

Michael even sang a lot at the hospital when he had pneumonia. But for some reason, he was never interested in singing much after that.

Well, I finally found out the answer to my riddles. Michael's best friend had a lot of ear infections and had tubes put in his

> *"My child is not a piece of clay that I can mold to my likes and dislikes; he is his own person and he is a person I love."*
>
> Beth Wilson Saavedra

91

"It has been said that there is no such thing as a problem that didn't have a gift in it."

ears. And so had a number of other children I knew. So I thought that maybe Michael just had fluid in his ears and took him to the pediatrician to find out. He said no, Michael's ears were just fine.

I was not convinced, so we went to an audiologist. I will never forget that day when this wonderfully sweet woman sat us down in her office to tell us our child had permanent hearing loss. Michael would have to wear hearing aids for the rest of his life. I was too shocked to be upset, but believe me, waves of grief set in later.

David was more matter-of-fact about it. He said we both wear glasses, and this is just like glasses only it's for the ears. He also said worse things could happen. I had to agree with both those points, but during the next several years I was still always looking for some way to correct Michael's hearing loss.

However, when we went to pick up the hearing aids a few weeks later, something really wonderful happened. This has to be one of the most touching experiences of my life. I'm getting misty just writing about it!

When the audiologist put the hearing aids on Michael for the very first time, he opened up his mouth and started to sing!

I couldn't believe it! I had been trying in round about ways to get him interested in singing for the past two years!

The way home in the van was no less exciting.

"Mommy, I can hear the van motor!"

"Mommy, I can hear you talking while the van is going!"

"Mommy, I can hear the cars on the street!"

Wow! What an awakening! There were some adjustments, of course. Michael's ears had to get used to the ear molds, and he had to get used to the hearing aids. They amplify everything, and I now know that people with hearing impairments have a lot of challenges to deal with.

Now that Michael is in first grade, he has a very understanding teacher. She has been more than willing to wear an FM system that amplifies her speech and transmits it to an antenna he wears. It's all under his clothes, so he doesn't look that different, which is important to him. It helps him hear her much better above the buzz in the classroom.

One time a couple weeks ago Michael came home from school, giggling proudly about an incident that had happened that day. He had been at the drinking fountain—completely out of his classroom with the door shut—when his teacher gave some instructions. With his antenna around his neck, he heard every

word she said and reentered the room, knowing what he was supposed to do next. He thought that was pretty slick—that he
heard it all and wasn't even in the room! For him it must have
felt wonderful, since I know there have been lots of times before
he got this system that his teacher was standing right there—and
he somehow wasn't understanding what he needed to know. It
was a constant source of frustration.

I now know that hearing-impaired children are often hyper-
active and easily frustrated—especially when their loss is not cor-
rected. That knowledge explains many incidents that happened
during the two years between the loss and its discovery—like
church behavior and his extreme frustration when, try as we
might, we couldn't understand what he was trying to tell us.

Today, although there are still some challenges, Michael
seems well-adjusted and we have accepted the loss. I can still get
teary-eyed when I watch him singing with all his heart—something he now really enjoys doing. But I feel like after a two-year
episode of worrying, wondering, and trying to understand so
many things, there is once again a song in our home.

Cari

REFLECTIONS

1. Some concerns you have for your child are . . .
2. A time you felt like singing was . . . because . . .
3. Something you got teary-eyed over recently was . . .
because . . .
4. God has given you a gift in your child in his or her . . .

*"Your
children
learn more
of your
faith during
the bad
times than
they do
during the
good
times."*

Beverly LaHaye

Chapter 22

THOSE WONDERFUL EXPECTATIONS

Dear Cari:

"Why do I get so little thanks for the many things I do that nobody wants done?"

Ashleigh Brilliant.

Thanks for sharing about Michael's singing. Now there's a song in my heart too! But a bit of an ache also, because of your loss and Michael's loss. I guess you never expected things to be quite this way!

Oh, those expectations! They'll reach out and grab you every time! Your letter got me to thinking about some of my expectations, and in my mind's eye I saw my two children—one was playing the flute, the other the French horn. That's what I had expected. And of course piano lessons would be a must. I made sure we had a piano in our home well before Marci or Ryan were ready for piano lessons. I wanted them to see the piano as a necessity of life—and of course, they would learn how to play it.

Admittedly I never became proficient at piano. As a child my best performances were for the letter carrier. When I was home and knew he was about to start up our steps, I would run to the piano and play "Home on the Range" just so he could hear me. I felt so important and capable! But when I was at my piano lesson, I felt anything but capable. It wasn't the teacher's fault. I just wished I could look at the music and play it. Learning fingering and timing wasn't much fun for me. In fact, it wasn't fun at all. Somehow I thought learning to play the piano should be fun! But I did get "Home on the Range" down pat. I already knew the words and the tune, so it was easier all the way around.

I wanted my children to do better! I also believed that if they learned the music of the great hymns and other gospel music that it would touch them deep down in their hearts and serve as protection for them as they grew older and were tempted to distance themselves from God and His promises. So we sang songs at worship (yes, I could play more than "Home on the Range"), and we sang in the car (we even had songbooks in the glove compartment). Ryan actually started piano lessons before Marci did, as I recall. I was so pleased and expectant!

94   Then we moved! And things didn't progress much after that.

Oh, both began lessons again, and I don't know if it could have been better or not, but neither was hooked on playing the piano. I tried all the tricks of the trade I knew to get them to practice without it becoming a battleground, but we finally decided the friction and frustration weren't worth it. But I still held out for the French horn and flute. I never forced my opinion, but I gave my children every option to take an instrument of their choice as they proceeded through grade school and even into high school. But they never took us up on our offers. I guess I'll hold out for heaven!

What I came to realize was that my expectation was really an illusion. I've learned that when reality sets in, it's often different than what I expected. We can be disillusioned and choose to separate from people emotionally and physically, handing out guilt and shame at their not meeting our expectations. Or we can adjust our hopes and attitudes. This has been quite a process for me, and I have to do it again and again, depending on the circumstances of my life! Regarding the music lessons, there have been some regret, guilt, and disappointment (and in relation to lots of family issues this isn't a real serious situation). I still feel somewhat sad that we aren't a more musical family. But these were *my* needs (not necessarily my talents or theirs), *my* wants (not necessarily my childrens').

"What we wish, that we readily believe."

Demosthenes

We all have many kinds of expectations of our children. I remember my mother-in-law saying that she wasn't sure who Ryan looked like, with his light brown hair and blue eyes—most of Don's family had *brown* eyes. Initially I was somewhat hurt and offended by her comment. Why, *I* had blue eyes, and *I* was his mother! But I realized that she wasn't being critical; rather, she was just adjusting to an unmet expectation. He didn't resemble their family as much as the other three grandchildren did. She loved all her grandchildren very much, and it was important for me to check out my own feelings and not project them on her.

Sometimes families are subtle about their expectations for their children, sometimes they aren't. I recall a college student who said she wished that her dad would recognize her as a young woman, not as his "buddy" anymore. She shared that she was the youngest of a family of all girls and that her dad was a farmer. She became his buddy as a child and fulfilled many of the expectations one would have of a boy. She helped more with chores, rode the tractor with him, etc. She enjoyed her place by his side as a child, but as she became older she longed for a father who could put his expectations for a boy aside and appreciate her for the woman she had become.

95

I recall another college student who sat in my office at the end of a quarter. She was trying to get the courage to tell her father that her love was children; she wanted to take a major to prepare her for teaching young children, rather than the premedical program she was enrolled in. We explored her options and her dreams, and she went home to talk to her father. At the beginning of the next quarter she came to tell me that she just couldn't stand up to her father. He had let her know that his children were to be physicians, and that was that!

Sometimes I haven't realized I had an expectation until it wasn't met! That's why it's so important that we be able to separate our feelings from our thinking and realize that when we have a certain emotional response that we need to stop and assess where it is coming from. Then we need to decide how we want to handle that feeling.

Back to Michael's hearing loss. His hearing impairment will still bring challenges, even though he is able to function quite well; and as you say, you have much to be thankful for. But I'm reminded, once again, that our lives have many opportunities for learning to adjust to our reality being different from our expectations. This means grieving, healing, and growing.

I well remember a noted speaker saying that it's very difficult for parents to complete the grieving process when children have profound disabilities. He suggested that each time parents look at the child, they will likely be reminded of the child they expected but didn't have.

We both have much to be thankful for. All four of our children can sing with all of their hearts—and they have many other wonderful traits and talents as well!

I close with a song in my heart!

Sue

P.S. I still do believe that when we teach our children the music, it will always be in their hearts. It reminds me of the text: "Thy word have I hid in mine heart, that I might not sin against thee" (Psalm 119:11, KJV).

FOUND IN MY FILES

"On his first visit to kindergarten, while mother was still with him, Bruce, age five, looked over the paintings on the wall and asked loudly, 'Who made these ugly pictures?' Mother was embarrassed. She looked at her son disapprovingly, and hastened to tell him, 'It's not nice to call the pictures ugly when they are so pretty.'

"The teacher, who understood the meaning of the question, smiled and said, 'In here you don't have to paint pretty pictures. You can paint mean pictures if you feel like it.' A big smile appeared on Bruce's face, for now he had the answer to his hidden question: 'What happens to a boy who doesn't paint so well?'

"Next Bruce picked up a broken fire engine and asked self-righteously, 'Who broke this fire engine?' Mother answered, 'What difference does it make to you who broke it? You don't know anyone here.'

"Bruce was not really interested in names. He wanted to find out what happened to boys who break toys. Understanding the question, the teacher gave an appropriate answer: 'Toys are for playing. Sometimes they get broken. It happens.'

"Bruce seemed satisfied. His interviewing skill had netted him the necessary information: 'This grownup is pretty nice. She does not get angry quickly, even when a picture comes out ugly or a toy is broken. I don't have to be afraid. It is safe to stay here.' Bruce waved good-bye to his mother and went over to the teacher to start his first day of kindergarten" (Haim G. Ginott, *Between Parent and Child*, pp. 22, 23).

FROM MY PERSPECTIVE

PRECIOUS BABY BLUE EYES
(A Mother's Day poem to my mom)

He has precious baby blue eyes,
Dimples cute and sweet,
Many ways to surprise
Me from welcome sleep.

He is cheery in the morning,
Cuddly soft at night,
Fussy without warning
Be it day or night.

I bathe him rather often,
Keep his bottom clean,

97

Feel my own heart soften,
At how much he means.

He is full of smiles and sweetness,
With that darling smirk,
But when it comes to neatness,
He makes a lot of work!

He keeps me oh so busy,
I don't know what to do,
I'm often in a tizzy—
My house looks like a zoo.

It makes me sometimes wonder
As I sneak a baby kiss,
Could this thought be a blunder,
Or was I once like this?

Did you cuddle me at midnight,
Keep me nice and clean,
Shield me from the sunlight
And dangers yet unseen?

Did you love me like I love him,
Feel the way I do,
Sometimes feel your eyes brim
With loving teardrops too?

You are my own dear mother,
You've done so much for me—
You've loved me like no other,
And now I clearly see,

When I look into those eyes of blue
I start to comprehend—
For I was once a part of you—
Yes, now I understand.

I love you, mom.
Happy Mother's Day!

Cari

REFLECTIONS

1. Are you concentrating on helping your children develop the traits, skills, and habits that will match God's interests in your children's lives? How?

2. What are some of your expectations that have been met in your children?

3. What are some of your expectations that have not been met in your children?

4. Where did you get the rules you have for how boys and/or girls should be, what your children should be like?

Chapter 23

PEACE AFTER THE STORM

Dear Sue,

We're spending the summer on the lake—in a friend's house with a cathedral ceiling. It's the nicest house I've ever stayed in, and the windows looking out over the lake seem enormous. They seemed even bigger during the huge storm we had last night.

I first noticed some ominous gray clouds overhead while I was splashing by the dock with Matthew and Michael. Their squeals of delight were soon interrupted by peals of thunder, and we decided to go inside.

Michael was none too happy about the decision, because he was having a great time, so I tried to explain. "A storm is coming, Michael. When there is thunder and lightning, the lake is not a good place to be."

We had scarcely gotten inside when some real outdoor theatrics began. The sky darkened into a still deeper gray, and fog settled in over the lake. The wind started whipping through our apartment, slamming doors and blowing papers. David and I rushed about closing sliding doors and windows.

The rain fell slowly at first then pelted down in sheets of fury. The drumbeat on the roof was relentless—its sound being broken only by louder and still louder peals of thunder along with the howling wind.

There is a wall of bay windows overlooking the lake here, and throughout the past week they've furnished us with a very restful view of the lake. But last night they were framing hurricane-style weather, and that made it all the more frightening.

David kept pacing around the house, which only confirmed my own feelings of apprehension. Lightning lit up the north shore of the lake again and again, illuminating wind-driven and angry waves on the lake. Subsequent bolts of lightning flashed all around us. Michael leaped onto my lap, where Matthew had already snuggled. With both boys nestled into my arms, I almost forgot the weather and started thinking about how sweet they were. Then a thought-altering, bone-jarring crash of thunder in-

> "Parenthood is a partnership with God. . . . You are working with the Creator of the universe in shaping human character and determining destiny."
>
> Ruth Vaughn

terrupted any thoughts of satisfaction I did have.

I clutched Michael and Matthew closer as the cover blew off our neighbors boat and the storm howled into a new level of fury. The rain pounded down for at least an hour before it began to lighten. The rolling thunder became gradually more distant, and lighting was flashing on the horizon only once more. The wind died down to a whimper, and fog lifted from the lake. Then there was a most welcome sight—the sun breaking through the clouds.

"Thank You, Lord," I couldn't help but whisper. We had sur-vived—tornado watches, tempestuous winds, and torrents of rain notwithstanding. Michael climbed tentatively off my lap. Pressing his nose against the window, he watched the neighbor draining his boat. I hugged Matthew tighter, then looked down at him in surprise. He was asleep! In the midst of the worst storm I had seen in years, complete with surround-sound thunder and continual lightning, he had slumbered off peacefully in my arms. A book had fallen into his crib, which I managed to pull out while laying him gently down. I couldn't help but smile as I looked at the cover, then back at his peaceful, sleeping face. *Worry-free Living* it read. That's what I want to have.

Cari

REFLECTIONS

1. What have been some of the storms in your life recently?
2. How did you react? With fear and apprehension? Or some other emotion?
3. Are there some lessons you can learn from your children about trust?

"Casting the whole of your care— all your anxieties, all your worries, all your concerns, once and for all—on Him; for He cares for you affectionately, and cares about you watchfully"

(1 Peter 5:7, Amplified).

101

Chapter 24

WHEN I BECAME A MOTHER

Dear Cari:

What a beautiful experience—peace after the storm! It really struck me that Matthew felt safe in your arms. He could trust his mother!

And that's what our children need from us the most. They need to trust us. Initially they need to trust us to meet their needs in infancy so that they can know they belong here on this earth. Then they need to trust us to understand how children develop and grow and to have confidence in them as individuals. They need to trust us to be consistent in our responses to them, to look for the positive, to take them as they are and love them as God gave them to us. They need to trust us with all their feelings, their fears, their questions, and their ideas.

They need to trust us to become all we can become as individuals, to keep growing, to put our own trust in the Lord. They need us to grow beyond our own childhoods, to be there for them as healthy adults.

They certainly don't need us to be perfect. How do you keep up with a perfect parent anyhow? But they need to trust us to make amends when we are impatient, shortsighted, or hurtful. They need to trust us to learn ways to communicate effectively with them, to discipline them in love—in other words, to give them nurture and structure.

They need us to share our journeys with them, to let them know how we find God, how we put our trust in Him in the midst of the storms of life on this earth. They need to trust that no matter what, they can count on us! The seeds of mature adult faith are planted very early as children relate within the family. A mother's love is vitally important! We should never underestimate our influence or significance in our children's lives. And I don't think that ever ends, it's a lifetime commitment!

And we don't need to have all the answers up front. We can grow as they grow. Motherhood is not a destination—it's a journey. It's a very personal journey, different from anyone else's.

I've been thinking about my own journey. Now, I didn't set out purposely to be a mother. I mean I wasn't one of those little girls who dreamed of the day she would have a real baby in her arms. I did play with dolls. That's what little girls were supposed to do, and I loved my dolls. They were my playmates, my friends, and I have them to this day. There was Patsy, whom I received on my first Christmas. She was nearly as big as I. Janet was one of my favorites. And of course, Judy, my Toni doll—oh, how many sugar-water perms did I give her! Yes, I loved my dolls, but I didn't long to be a mother.

Actually, I wasn't around babies much as a child, and I really didn't know what to do with them. One summer night, when I was in college, I was asked to take care of two little children whose parents wanted to go to the fair. Shortly after they left, someone knocked on the door—a stranger at the door. I could see a pickup truck by the curb, and inside sat a woman with a baby in her arms. He told me that his friends said I would take care of their baby while they went to the fair too. What was I to say? (I'd never been given permission to say no to much of anything, so why start now?) So in they came—mother, baby, bottle, and diaper bag. When I saw how little the infant was, I asked, "How old is she?"

As the mother plopped her in my arms, she responded, "Oh, she's almost 2 weeks old!"

And off they went. And there I was with two toddlers and an infant, none of whom I knew what to do with! I hadn't even held a baby that young before. I put her on the bed and wondered what to do with her next. Yes, I too was somewhat astounded that they would leave her with a total stranger, but I managed to care for all three of them just fine that night.

Then life went on. Don and I married. We got teased about when we were going to have children. And life went on some more. We both wanted children eventually—but not yet. We had been married about three years when some friends of ours went to look at a possible teaching position out of state. They asked—or maybe we offered—but at any rate we took care of their baby girl, Lori, for almost a week. She was just as precious as a little girl could be at 5 months! I remember dressing her up for church and how she snuggled in my arms as I held her once we got there. (Whew, that wasn't quick or easy—getting there.) I also remember all the knowing looks we were getting. Some other childless friends were keeping Lori's 1-and-a-half-year-old brother, Scott, and I saw people smile as they came into church with him too. Anyway, the next day when we put her into bed with us to cuddle and play, I was just overwhelmed with the deep, settled feeling that this was right for us. I was ready to be a parent! And Don was certain too. Well, as certain as he could be, in contemplating this business of parenthood.

To get to the point, we took the leap and Marci was born in about record time. As we were driving home from the hospital when she was a few days old, we stopped for a traffic light. As I looked out my car window, a big, burly man was smiling down at me from a big truck. Marci was in my arms, so I pulled the blanket back so that he could see her face, and he waved at us. I was touched by his pleasure! I was struck with the realization, "Wow, he thinks this is pretty special—it is—I'm a mother!"

And I didn't know much about being a mother. There were few books or magazine articles about parenting and child behavior those days! If I had known then what I know now, I would have been more intimidated by the heavy responsibilities ahead, but I thoroughly enjoyed this new thing called motherhood.

Oh, let me tell you a little more about Lori. Lori will always hold a special place in our hearts, not just because she was so precious but also because she was the catalyst to our choosing to build our family then. Had we not made the choice at that time, even though we would have had *a* child, it would not have been Marci! I'll never be able to tell Lori about her special place in our hearts, because she lost her life in a tragic accident as a young high school student. Telling her mother that caring for Lori convinced us to become parents has given me some comfort, however.

I have thoroughly enjoyed motherhood. Our two children have brought untold joy and happiness to our lives. That's not to say there haven't been sleepless nights (when they were babies, as well as when they were teens—and a few times in between), unanswered questions in my mind as to what I should have done differently or better, and moments of real sadness as I've realized that I've hurt or misunderstood them or realized that their childhood has passed and whatever I did or didn't do can't be changed.

Although I am no longer responsible *for* them, I will always remain responsible *to* them.

But being a mother has been a very important part in my search to become as emotionally healthy, informed, and produc-

tive as I can be. No, I didn't meet all their needs. No one individual can do that for another. But I remain committed to them.
I have put my trust in the Lord for my sake, as well as theirs.

And I'm anticipating the rest of the journey. It's such a privilege to know our children as adults! (Yes, you'll get there too!)
They are responsible, resourceful, loving human beings, each
uniquely himself or herself. They are on their own—sometimes
difficult—journeys. Michele, Ryan's wife, and Michael, Marci's
husband, are very special to us. (I always thought the ideal was
two girls and two boys!) Recently I sat in the congregation as
Michael sang a solo for the church service. His clear tenor voice
sang, "Lord, I want to be a Christian in my heart . . ." As I lis-
tened to the words of each stanza, there was such clear meaning
for me that my heart filled and tears came to my eyes. Not only
was I compelled to recommit to those words myself, but I felt
blessed to have a son-in-law with that commitment to God. All
will be blessed, including Marci and their new daughter,
Cassandra Elizabeth!—our first grandchild!

May our journey always be in the same direction, side-by-side.

Sue

REFLECTIONS

1. How has God used your experience as a mother to put
your trust in Him?

2. Some of your greatest joys in the journey of motherhood are . . .

3. Some of your greatest concerns in this journey are . . .

4. Places where you get or can get support in this journey
are . . .

5. When your children are grown, you . . .

Dear Readers:

This book was not written with the intention of giving expert parenting advice or covering all the concerns of parenting and mothering. We've just shared parts of our journeys—two mothers who are at different stages of life and who care about each other—and other mothers as well.

We leave you with these thoughts:

"May he give you the desire of your heart and make all your plans succeed. We will shout for joy when you are victorious and will lift up our banners in the name of our God. . . . Some trust in chariots and some in horses, but we trust in the name of the Lord our God" (Ps. 20:4-7, NIV).

"May the God of hope fill you with joy and peace in your faith, that by the power of the Holy Spirit, your whole life and outlook may be radiant with hope" (Rom. 15:13, Phillips).

Cari and Sue

How to Help Your Child Really Love Jesus

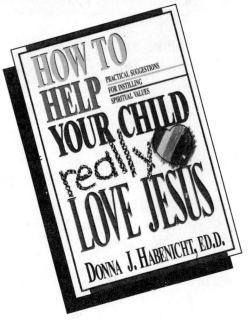

Here are hundreds of practical ideas from child development specialist Donna J. Habenicht for helping your child grow spiritually. Special features include:

- faith development tasks for early and late childhood
- description of the four main parenting styles
- scale of the nine temperament traits found in most children
- Bible study developmental tasks
- a spiritual development chart
- Sabbath activity ideas for all ages
- family helping projects
- worship activities appropriate for different ages.

Paper, 224 pages.
US$11.99, Cdn$16.20.

In Praise of Children

Poems and Quotes
Compiled and edited by Kay Kuzma

A delightful treasury of poems and quotes ideal for baby dedications, home dedications, Mother's Day, Father's Day, Grandparents Day, and other family celebrations. Or simply for savoring the joy and fulfillment brought by having children in your life.

Topics: ❖ Baby ❖ Girls ❖ Boys ❖ Grandparents ❖ Character ❖ Home ❖ Children ❖ Hugs ❖ Christmas ❖ Mothers ❖ Family ❖ Parents ❖ Fathers

Paper, US$10.99, Cdn$14.85.

THE
LADDER
OF LIFE
SERIES

Help your children develop the Christian virtues mentioned by Peter in 2 Peter (faith, virtue, temperance, patience, love, etc.) by using The Ladder of Life *Activity and Song Book*, storybooks, and cassettes.

As your children listen to the character-building stories, sing the delightful songs, and engage in the creative learning activities, they'll develop a friendship with Jesus and a desire to reflect His character.

Activity and Song Book

Contains learning activities that range in complexity for ages birth through early elementary, memory verses that reinforce the character traits, songs with easy-to-play piano accompaniment, and discussion questions. Paper, US$9.99, Cdn$13.50.

Storybooks

Eight storybooks for children based on the character traits in 2 Peter 1:5-7. Each story is about 5-6 pages long. The pictures can be colored. Paper, US$3.99, Cdn$5.40 each.

Activity and Song Book and eight storybooks
US$39.99, Cdn$54.00.

Cassettes

Feature the same stories as the storybooks and songs that reinforce the virtues. A tone tells the child when to turn the page of the storybook if he or she chooses to follow along. Four cassettes. Coming soon.

Journal of a Happy Woman

by June Strong

IN THIS CLASSIC that has inspired a generation of readers Mrs. Strong shares her family (six children, four of them adopted), her joys, her frustrations, and her victories—a year from her life.

Favorite recipes, poetry, a tour of Elm Valley Farm—including the special delight of a hidden prayer corner created from a weed patch—all weave together to form a book few women will be able to resist.

Down to earth, practical, and spiritual, yet whimsical and funny, June Strong's book clamors to be read, cherished, and brought out again to reread when you need laughter or encouragement.

This edition updates readers on her life since this book was first published 21 years ago. Paper, 155 pages. US$9.99, Cdn$13.50.